CAN A DEAD MAN STRIKE OUT?

offbeat
baseball
questions
and their
improbable
answers

Mark S. Halfon

SANTA
MONICA
PRESS

Published by:
Santa Monica Press LLC
P.O. Box 1076
Santa Monica, CA 90406-1076
1-800-784-9553
www.santamonicapress.com
books@santamonicapress.com

Printed in the United States

Santa Monica Press books are available at special quantity discounts when purchased in bulk by corporations, organizations, or groups. Please call our Special Sales department at 1-800-784-9553.

Library of Congress Cataloging-in-Publication Data

Halfon, Mark S.
    Can a dead man strike out? : offbeat baseball questions and their improbable answers / by Mark S. Halfon.
        p. cm.
    Includes bibliographical references and index.
    ISBN 1-891661-49-3
    1. Baseball—United States—Miscellanea. I. Title.
    GV873.H25 2005
    796.357—dc22

                                                    2004029790

Cover photo by C Squared Studios/Getty Images
Author photo by Steve Richman
Cover design by Susan Landesmann
Interior design by Lynda "Cool Dog" Jakovich

Contents

Dedication

For Melissa and Jesse, Vicki and Jacob

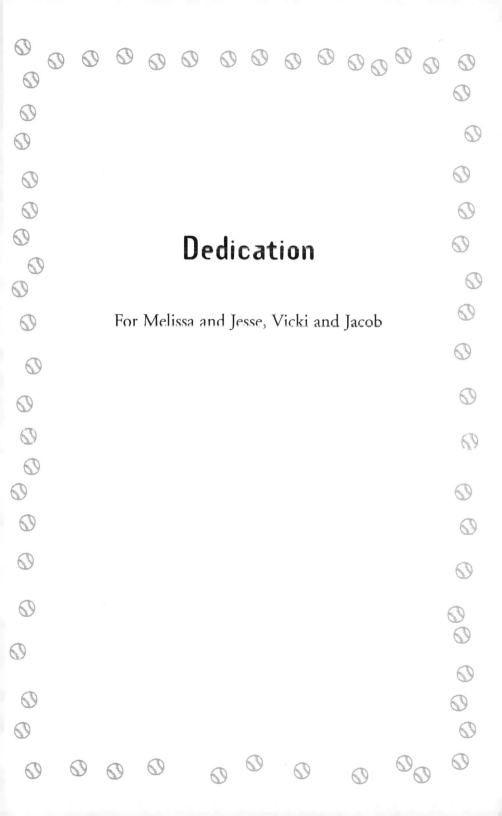

Acknowledgments

Baseball connects generations. My father, Victor, used to take me to see the Brooklyn Dodgers play at Ebbets Field. I've attended many games with my son Jesse and daughter Melissa, and have no doubt their children will experience the joy of baseball. But it was Jesse's entry into Little League and his love of baseball which inspired a book that has been nearly 20 years in the making. It's been so long I can barely remember when I started, but it began with offbeat questions to Jesse. Years went by as I jotted down additional questions and anecdotes.

My son Jesse's passion for baseball inspired *Can a Dead Man Strike Out?*, but his contribution to the book goes well beyond inspiration. Jesse's appreciation of the nuances of baseball kept my imagination at full throttle. His understanding of my distaste for "trivial" trivia was a constant reminder of pitfalls to be avoided. Jesse's editorial comments vastly improved the quality of the writing, and some of the questions in the book come from his fertile imagination.

Special thanks to fellow philosopher and baseball aficionado Ken Shouler, whose insights and advice helped turn a manuscript into a book. Ken has published numerous sports books and he provided invaluable advice on the winding road to publication. A friend and writer, Tom Martinson, meticulously scrutinized the manuscript and offered numerous suggestions. Many of his recommendations were incorporated into the text.

Assists go to David W. Anderson, Bill Atkins, Yvette Bachmeier, Melissa Halfon, Nancy Halfon, Sid Hochman, Alan Kluger, John Lango, Phil Olsen, Phil Pecorino, Angel Perez, Larry Rapaport, Steve Richman and Marcela Roy for their encouragement, friendship and love. Special thanks to Melissa for her contribution to the question about Jim Abbott. Let me add my love to Loretta, who turned me into a Brooklyn Dodgers fan. I'm also indebted to the Society for American Baseball Research (www.sabr.org). Their daily online discussion group, SABR-L, was a guide throughout my research.

Two outstanding online baseball sites proved of incalculable worth. They are the Baseball Almanac (www.baseball-almanac.com) and Retrosheet (www.retrosheet.org). Each site has a wealth of reliable information. I'd also thank W.C. Burdick, manager of photo services at the National Baseball Hall of Fame.

Lastly, thanks to publisher Jeffrey Goldman, who put the finishing touches on *Can a Dead Man Strike Out?*

William "Dummy" Hoy, a deaf mute, was one of the premiere outfielders at the turn of the 20th century. Legend has it that his disability caused umpires to use hand and arm signals when calling balls and strikes. (National Baseball Hall of Fame Library, Cooperstown, NY)

Introduction

"People ask me what I do in winter when there is no baseball. I'll tell you what I do. I stare out the window and wait for spring."
—Rogers Hornsby

Baseball is an unpredictable game. Unusual plays can happen virtually any time during a game. *Can a Dead Man Strike Out?* is focused on offbeat events that have occurred or might occur in the course of a baseball season.

- Is it possible for a team to have the best record in baseball without making the playoffs?
- Can a pitcher win a game without throwing a pitch?
- Was there an American League pitcher who never played in a major league game?
- Can a player score a run without being in the game?

The answer to every one of these questions is "yes," and each event happened.

Every answer takes the form of a narrative that puts the event into context. Some of the game's more memorable events and stories—typically with an unlikely twist—are the focus of most questions. Special attention is paid to baseball records and feats that have been ignored or forgotten but nonetheless deserve recognition. Virtually all of the records mentioned in the book cover the modern era, which began in 1903 when the

National League and American League merged to form the major leagues.

Each question and answer function as a unit to tell a story about a substantive aspect of the game. Often the question and answer should be read together. Virtually every narrative attempts to capture a glimpse of the culture and history of baseball. In many cases, the point of a passage is to make the reader aware of some magical moment in baseball history. In other cases, the challenge is to figure out how certain events could happen. In all instances, the purpose is to enjoy and appreciate the subtleties of a game that continues to evoke wonder.

Can a Dead Man Strike Out? is as likely to mention the achievements of Urban Shocker, Iceberg Chamberlain, and Henry Mathewson as those of Babe Ruth, Ted Williams, and Christy Mathewson. Baseball historians, statisticians, trivia buffs, die-hard fans, and the inquisitive will have their understanding of baseball rules, records and history challenged. Get ready to journey down the traveled road of baseball.

— Mark S. Halfon
February 2005

Ty Cobb's unorthodox split-hand grip contributed to his major league best .366 career average. Also, notice the position of the catcher. During the Deadball Era, catchers stood in a crouch position a couple of feet behind home plate.
(National Baseball Hall of Fame Library, Cooperstown, NY)

Chapter One

Batter Up!

*"I keep my eyes clear, and I hit 'em
where they ain't."*
—Wee Willie Keeler

Home Runs

Who took the longest to hit his first home run?

Dozens of batters have homered in their first major league game. More often players wait weeks, months, or years, but no one has waited as long as Johnny Cooney to record his first home run. Cooney was a left-handed pitcher for the Boston Braves from 1921 through 1930. He had a career best 14 victories in 1925, but arm problems plagued him at the end of the season. An operation intended to correct the problem left Cooney's pitching arm a couple of inches shorter than the other. He managed to win only eight games in the ensuing five years and was forced into retirement from 1931 to 1934.

Cooney's career was far from over, though—he reinvented himself as an outfielder. After having successfully developed his hitting skills in the minor leagues, Brooklyn Dodgers manager Casey Stengel returned him to the majors in 1935. Cooney was an effective hitter for the Dodgers over the next two years, but he was traded to the St. Louis Cardinals for Leo "The Lip" Durocher at the close of the 1937 season. Prior to the start of the '38 season, Cooney moved on to the Boston Bees. On September 24, 1939, the Bees visited the New York Giants at the Polo Grounds, and Cooney drilled his first major league homer. It took the resilient ballplayer 18 years to reach that coveted milestone.

How long did Cooney have to wait for his next round-tripper? One day! He homered in his very next game. Those were Cooney's only home runs in a career that spanned more than two decades.

⚾ ⚾ ⚾

What are the most home runs hit by a player in one day?

A few batters have slammed four home runs in a game, but that's not the record for homers in one day. On May 2, 1954, St. Louis Cardinals outfielder Stan "The Man" Musial slammed three home runs in the opener of a doubleheader against the visiting New York Giants, but he wasn't done yet. Musial added two homers in the nightcap, becoming the first player in baseball history to hit five round-trippers in one day.

The Cardinals' star was one of baseball's all-time great hitters and was inducted into the Hall of Fame in 1969.

Musial's record-setting performance was seen by eight-year-old Nate Colbert, who was in the stands at Sportsman's Park. Twelve years later, Colbert broke into the major leagues with the Houston Astros. By 1972 the big first baseman was playing with the San Diego Padres. On August 1 of that season, the Padres visited Atlanta's Fulton County Stadium to play a doubleheader against the Braves. Colbert went 4-for-5 with two homers and five RBIs in the opener, but he outdid himself in the second game, going 3-for-4 with three home runs and eight RBIs. His 13 RBIs established a major league record.

Colbert became only the second player in baseball history to hit five homers in a day, tying a record he witnessed 18 years earlier.

⚾ ⚾ ⚾

What are the fewest home runs by a team in one season?

It had to be a team that played during the Deadball Era (1901 to 1919), when the quality of the baseball made it virtually impossible to consistently hit home runs. Among the weakest hitting squads of the time were the Chicago White Sox. Despite a .230 team average and a mere seven round-trippers, the original "Hitless Wonders" took home the 1906 AL pennant. Not to be undone, the 1907 White Sox managed to register only five home runs.

But it was the 1908 Chisox who set the all-time low with exactly three homers (compare that with the fact that about a dozen batters have hit four home runs in a single game).

Home run production increased for the 1909 White Sox as they registered four home runs. Nineteen home runs by one team over four consecutive years is barely imaginable by contemporary standards. Cub's slugger Sammy Sosa had more four-baggers in one month alone, connecting on 20 round trippers in June, 1998.

⚾ ⚾ ⚾

Who took six weeks to hit four consecutive home runs?

On July 17, 1990, Kansas City Royals centerfielder Bo Jackson hit three home runs in his first three at-bats off New York Yankees right-hander Andy Hawkins. Jackson would have had an opportunity to hit his fourth homer in a row except for the following play: Yankees leadoff man Deion Sanders hit a sinking line drive toward centerfield in the sixth inning. Jackson attempted a diving catch, but the ball went past him as Sanders flew around the bases to score an inside-the-park home run. Unfortunately, Jackson separated a shoulder on the play and was denied a chance to hit a fourth consecutive homer that day.

The Royals centerfielder was placed on the disabled list for almost six weeks. On August 26 Jackson returned to action against the Seattle Mariners. In his first at-bat since the injury, Jackson connected on a two-run homer off Mariners lefty Randy Johnson. The Royals slugger tied a major league record with his fourth consecutive home run. A handful of batters have accomplished this feat, but Jackson is the only one to have done so over such an extended period.

Jackson and Sanders were both outstanding football players who excelled in the collegiate ranks as well as the National Football League. Jackson was a running back for the Los Angeles Raiders, but his football career was cut short by an injury he suffered during an NFL playoff game in 1991. He attempted a return to baseball in 1993 and hit a home run in his first at-bat since the unfortunate incident, but the injury took its toll. Jackson retired from baseball in 1994.

⚾ ⚾ ⚾

What were the most home runs hit in a season by Frank "Home Run" Baker?

Philadelphia Athletics third baseman Frank Baker played during the Deadball Era and was one of the dominant power hitters of his day. Baker led or tied for the American League lead in homers from 1911 to 1914. His career high came in 1913 when he slammed 12 home runs. Baker hit 96 home runs and batted .307 in his 13-year career.

His numbers might have been more impressive had he not missed two full seasons. Baker sat out the 1915 season due to a contract dispute with Athletics owner Connie Mack, and the 1920 season because his wife passed away and he stayed home to care for his two young children. In 1955 the Veterans Committee elected Baker to the Hall of Fame.

The Athletics slugger earned his nickname against the New York Giants in the 1911 World Series. Legendary hurler Christy Mathewson won the opener of the Series for the Giants. In Game Two the teams were tied 1–1, but the Athletics had a runner on base with two out in the bottom of the sixth inning when Baker hit a home run off southpaw Rube Marquard. The Athletics won the game 3–1, and tied the series at a game apiece.

Game Three turned into a pitchers' duel between Mathewson and Athletics ace right-hander Jack Coombs. Mathewson took a 1–0 lead into the ninth inning when Baker slammed a one-out homer to tie the contest. The Athletics went on to win in 11 innings and took a 2–1 series lead. From that day on Frank would be known as "Home Run" Baker. His home runs were especially impressive given that only one other four-bagger was hit in the entire Series. The Athletics won the 1911 World Series in six games.

⚾ ⚾ ⚾

Did Ty Cobb ever lead the league in home runs?

The "Georgia Peach" has the highest career average of any major league ballplayer in the history of the game. Cobb retired in 1928 with a .366 average over his 24-year career, including three .400 seasons. But Cobb's style of play diminished any chance of him hitting a great many homers. His objective was to get on a base and come around to score on a sacrifice, steal, hit and run or whatever else was necessary. Consequently, he used a split-hand grip that gave him greater bat control, but considerably reduced his power. Despite the grip, Cobb hit nine homers for the Detroit Tigers in 1909 to lead the American League for the one and only home run title of his career.

Although Cobb led the league in homers that season, he didn't hit a single ball out of the park. Each and every one of Cobb's four-baggers was an inside-the-park home run.

How many players have hit home runs in their first two at-bats of their first game?

Dozens of players have hit homers in their first major league at-bats, but St. Louis Browns rookie Bob Nieman had an even more impressive start to his career. The Browns faced the Boston Red Sox on September 14, 1951, and Nieman hit a home run in each of his first two at-bats. He might have homered for a third time, but chose to bunt in his third at-bat and did so safely. Nieman is the first and only player to hit back-to-back home runs in his first two at-bats of his first game.

Didn't St. Louis Cardinals rookie Keith McDonald accomplish the same feat? Not exactly. McDonald was called up from the minor leagues in the summer of 2000 to replace the Cardinals' injured catcher. His first major league at-bat was on July 4, and he slammed a pinch-hit home run against the Cincinnati Reds. His next plate appearance was two days later on July 6, also against the Reds, and he homered once again. So McDonald was the second player in major league history to hit homers in his first two at-bats, but it took him two games.

⚾ ⚾ ⚾

How many players have a first-inning pinch-hit home run?

Right-handed pitchers have a decided advantage against right-handed batters, and left-handed pitchers have that same edge against left-handed hitters. On May 24, 1947, Philadelphia Phillies manager Ben Chapman started right-hander Al Jurish for the sole purpose of pitching to Brooklyn Dodgers right-handed hitters Pee Wee Reese and Jackie Robinson. Chapman already had left-hander Oscar Judd warming up in the bullpen to face Pete Reiser, Dixie Walker and Gene Hermanski, all of whom were left-handed batters.

Despite Chapman's strategy, the Dodgers managed to get two runners on base with two out as Hermanski was scheduled to bat. But Dodgers manager Burt Shotton countered Chapman's moves and sent in right-handed pinch-hitter Carl Furillo. Furillo responded with a three-run homer, becoming the first and only player in baseball history with a first-inning pinch-hit home run.

Although Furillo pinch-hit that day in May, he was the regular right fielder during the glory days of the Dodgers. He was a superb hitter throughout his career, but his most significant contribution to the team was in the field. The "Reading Rifle" played the high right field wall in Ebbets Field as well as anyone, and he had a gun for an arm. He would stand at home plate prior to a game and throw the ball more than 400 feet over the center field fence. Furillo retired with a lifetime average near .300, including more than a thousand RBIs.

Who hit four home runs in four official at-bats in four games?

The key word here is "official" and a base on balls is not an official at-bat. The player who hit the four homers actually had 15 plate appearances during his streak, but he walked 11 times. Who did it? It was none other than Boston Red Sox great Ted Williams. The "Splendid Splinter" hit the first of his four homers in Boston's Fenway Park on September 18, 1957. The next three Red Sox games were on the road against the New York Yankees and Williams connected for a home run in each of those contests. The slugger managed to connect on four homers in four official at-bats over four games.

Williams finished the season with a .388 batting average, including 38 home runs. Although he had a spectacular season, some sportswriters were less than impressed with his performance. Williams had a strained relationship with the press, and that apparently played a role in the decision of two Chicago sportswriters to place Williams in ninth and 10th place respectively on their ballots for the American League MVP. As a result, Williams was edged out for the award by Yankees center fielder Mickey Mantle. Red Sox owner Tom Yawkey indignantly complained that some sportswriters were "incompetent and unqualified."

Which pitcher entered a game as a defensive replacement and hit two inside-the-park home runs?

On May 8, 1906, Philadelphia Athletics manager Connie Mack needed a substitute left fielder in the sixth inning of a game against the Boston Pilgrims. Unfortunately, Mack was shorthanded as a result of injuries to a number of his players. So the legendary skipper decided to bring in pitcher Charles "Chief" Bender, who happened to have hit the first home run of his major league career three days earlier. Bender rewarded Mack's confidence in him as he slammed two inside-the-park homers. Those home runs were noteworthy given that Bender hit only three more round-trippers in his 16-year career.

Bender got his nickname because he was part Chippewa Indian. Other Native American ballplayers were called "Chief," but not all were pleased with the reference to their ethnicity. In those days many Native Americans had their careers cut short by prejudice, but Bender became a dominant pitcher for the Athletics from 1903 to 1914. He retired at the end of the 1917 season with 212 victories and a 2.46 ERA. In 1953 the Veterans Committee elected Bender to the Hall of Fame.

Who was the first National Leaguer to hit two grand slam home runs in a game?

The National League has had its share of great hitters, but it took a pitcher to first accomplish this rare display of power. Atlanta Braves right-hander Tony Cloninger surprised San Francisco pitchers on July 3, 1966, hitting two grand slam home runs. He also drove in nine runs for the game, establishing a major league record for pitchers. Cloninger broke the NL mark of five RBIs, which was held by many, including Cloninger himself, who had tied the record only two weeks earlier.

On April 23, 1999, St. Louis Cardinals third baseman Fernando Tatis became the second NL player to hit two grand slam homers in one game, but Tatis hit his grand slam home runs in the same inning. Los

Angeles Dodgers right-hander Chan Ho Park gave up both round-trippers, becoming the only pitcher in the modern era to surrender two grand slam homers in an inning. Tatis set two major league records in the game. First, he's the only player with two grand slam home runs in an inning. Second, no one else has had as many as eight RBIs in one inning.

Which father and son hit back-to-back home runs?

Quite a few father/son tandems have played major league baseball, but only one of the duos managed to hit consecutive homers. Ken Griffey Sr. was traded to the Seattle Mariners late in the 1990 season. He joined his son, Ken Griffey Jr. They became the first father and son to play as teammates. On September 14, the Mariners were on the road facing right-hander Kirk McCaskill and the California Angels. In the top of the first inning, McCaskill gave up a leadoff base on balls, which was followed by a two-run homer by Griffey Sr. "Junior" batted next and slammed his 20th round-tripper of the year. No other father and son have hit back-to-back home runs.

Which Hall of Famer hit the only home run of his 21-year career in his first at-bat?

New York Giants rookie right-hander Hoyt Wilhelm made his major league debut on April 23, 1952. Wilhelm pitched five innings in relief against the Boston Braves and recorded his first major league victory. He also contributed at the plate, hitting a home run in his first major league at-bat. Wilhelm went on to have a lengthy and impressive career, eventually retiring in 1972. He played in 1,007 games in his 21-year career, but never hit another homer.

Wilhelm became one of the great relief pitchers in baseball history. His trademark knuckleball baffled hitters year after year. At the time of his retirement, Wilhelm set career records for most games pitched, relief wins, innings pitched in relief, games pitched in relief and games finished by a pitcher. Imagine if he didn't spend seven years in the minor leagues. In 1985 Wilhelm became the first relief pitcher inducted into the Hall of Fame.

Hits and More Hits

Who got a base hit for two different teams in two different cities on the same day?

Either a little imagination or knowledge of Joel Youngblood's career will be needed to figure out how this could happen. For much of the 1982 season, New

York Mets manager George Bamberger was upset with a number of his players, including Youngblood, who were thought to be a constant source of disharmony in the clubhouse. On August 4 the Mets visited Chicago's Wrigley Field to play an afternoon game against the Cubs. Youngblood went 1-for-2, driving in two runs with a third-inning single against right-hander Ferguson Jenkins. That would be his final at-bat for the Mets.

Youngblood was traded in the middle of the game to the Montreal Expos, who were scheduled to play an evening road contest against the Philadelphia Phillies. When told he was traded, Youngblood left the stadium, headed to the airport and flew to Philadelphia. He arrived at Veterans Stadium shortly after the game started and came in to play right field in the bottom of the sixth inning. In the top of the seventh Youngblood singled against southpaw Steve Carlton. Youngblood managed to get a base hit for two different teams in two different cities on the same day—and he did it against two future Hall of Famers.

⚾ ⚾ ⚾

Did anyone bat .400 as a rookie?

"Shoeless Joe" Jackson broke into the big leagues with the Philadelphia Athletics in 1908 and played a total of 30 games over the next three seasons. Athletics manager Connie Mack traded him to the Cleveland Naps in 1910. Jackson's first full season was in 1911 when he batted .408 in 147 games for the Naps. Although the young right fielder was not considered a rookie at the time, he would qualify as one based on today's rules.

Despite Jackson's outstanding season, he finished second in the batting race to the legendary Ty Cobb. Jackson went on to become one of the great hitters in the game. He batted .356 for his career, third best in the history of baseball. "Shoeless Joe" seemed destined for greatness, but his career was cut short as a result of his involvement in the infamous "Black Sox Scandal."

Jackson was playing with the Chicago White Sox in 1919 and led his team to an American League Championship. As the 1919 World Series was about to begin, rumors spread that the Series had been fixed. It turned out that the Cincinnati Red Legs would "upset" the highly regarded White Sox. Rumors persisted throughout the 1920 season about the involvement of White Sox players, including Shoeless Joe. On September 28, 1920, an Illinois Grand Jury indicted Jackson and seven of his teammates.

As a result of the public inquiry, it became known that the eight players were alleged to have taken bribes to throw the 1919 World Series. The players involved may have been vulnerable since they were furious with White Sox owner Charles Comiskey. Comiskey apparently reneged on a promise to give bonuses to a number of players for winning the 1917 World Series. Members of the White Sox team also felt that Comiskey paid disproportionately low salaries.

Eventually sympathetic jurors acquitted all the players for rigging the series, but the joy of the White Sox players was short-lived. Judge Kenesaw Mountain Landis, the first commissioner of baseball, had recently come to power as a result of corruption in the game. Landis was given a lifetime contract with a mandate to clean up baseball. On the day after the jury acquittal, the newly empowered commissioner ruled that Jackson and seven of his teammates were involved in an attempt to rig the 1919 World Series, and he banned the players from baseball for life. "Shoeless Joe" had played his last game.

Which brothers finished first and second in a batting race?

The Alou family has had its share of big league ballplayers. Brothers Felipe, Jesus, and Matty each had lengthy major league careers. Moises, son of Felipe, has been a four-time National League All-Star. Right-hander Mel Rojas is Moises's cousin and nephew of the three brothers. The Alou clan has made its mark in baseball over the years, but Matty and Felipe managed a deed unparalleled in baseball history when they took the top two spots in a batting race. Matty played for the Pittsburgh Pirates in 1966 and won the NL batting title with a .342 average. Felipe, who played for the Atlanta Braves that season, came in second with a .327 average. No other brother tandem has accomplished this feat.

Another rarity occurred on September 10, 1963, when all three Alou brothers batted consecutively in the same inning for the same team. San Francisco Giants manager Alvin Dark sent Jesus, Matty, and Felipe to the plate in the top of the eighth inning. Notably, it was Jesus's major league debut.

⚾ ⚾ ⚾

Which team scored 11 runs in an inning on only one hit?

The 1906 Chicago White Sox excelled despite the absence of a potent offense. They managed to win the American League pennant that season with an anemic .228 team average. It was the lowest team batting average for any pennant winner, giving credence to their richly deserved nickname "The Hitless Wonders." The White Sox team of the late 1950s also achieved success on the diamond without a powerful lineup. No game, or rather, inning better exemplified their reputation than one against the Kansas City Athletics on April 22, 1959. The Athletics took an early 6–1 lead in the contest, but the visiting White Sox roared back.

In the top of the seventh inning, the first two White Sox batters, Ray Boone and Al Smith, each reached base on an error. Johnny Callison followed with the only hit of the inning—an RBI single that scored Boone. Athletics right fielder Roger Maris booted Callison's ball and allowed Smith to score on the play as well. After the next two batters walked, Athletics reliever Mark Freeman entered the game. The right-hander gave up two more bases on balls before getting Jim Landis for the first out of the inning. Freeman walked yet another White Sox batter and was relieved by left-hander George Brunet.

The wildness of the Athletics pitching staff continued. Brunet gave up two more base on balls, hit Callison, and walked Luis Aparicio before striking out the opposing pitcher for the second out of the inning. With the bases loaded and nine runs having crossed the plate, Brunet walked two more batters, allowing runs 10 and 11 to score. Finally, Landis grounded out for the second time in the inning to end the carnage. The White Sox scored 11 runs on one hit, three errors, 10 walks, and one hit batsman as they crushed the Athletics 20–6.

The White Sox won the American League pennant in 1959.

⚾ ⚾ ⚾

Who doubled into a double play?

The Brooklyn Dodgers, who were called the Brooklyn Robins from 1914 to 1931, faced the Boston Braves in the opener of a doubleheader on August 15, 1926. In the first game of the twin bill, the Robins had the bases loaded and one out with Chick Fewster on first base, Dazzy Vance on second and Hank DeBerry on third. Robins rookie Babe Herman came to the plate and drove the ball deep against the right field wall, easily scoring DeBerry on the play. Vance was heading home, but he decided to reverse course and headed back to third base.

Fewster was already standing on the third base bag. Herman then joined his teammates on third as he attempted to stretch a double into a triple. The Robins ended up with three runners on third base!

The Braves third baseman tagged Vance and Herman, but Vance was entitled to third base since he was the lead runner. Herman was ruled out for passing Fewster on the base path, but Fewster mistakenly thought both runners were ruled out and he left the bag believing the inning was over. Fewster was then tagged out to officially end the inning. Herman was charged with hitting into a double play, but he also was credited with a double for having reached second base safely. Somehow the team from Brooklyn won the game.

⚾ ⚾ ⚾

Who had the same batting average, home runs, and RBIs in two consecutive seasons?

The chance of hitting the same number of homers in consecutive years is small. The likelihood of having the same amount of home runs and RBIs in back-to-back seasons is extremely low. The probability of having the same numbers in homers, RBIs, and batting average in consecutive seasons is microscopic. Nonetheless, Colorado Rockies third baseman Vinny Castilla managed to do it, putting up impressive statistics in the process. Castilla batted .304 with 40 home runs and 113 RBIs in 1996 and again in 1997. Castilla is the only major leaguer to have the same batting average, homers, and RBIs in consecutive seasons.

Batting Records

Who got an RBI 65 years after he retired?

In 1930 Chicago Cubs slugger Hack Wilson set a single-season major league record of 190 RBIs. Wilson retired from baseball in 1934 with a .307 average, 244 homers, and 1,062 RBIs. But his RBI total would change many years later. In 1994 an observant sportswriter discovered a scoring error that deprived Wilson of an additional RBI. The contested RBI came from the second game of a doubleheader against the Cincinnati Reds on July 28, 1930. Wilson's teammate Charlie Grimm was credited with two RBIs and Wilson with none, but each should have been credited with one RBI.

Commissioner Bud Selig corrected the error on June 28, 1999, and approved a change in Wilson's RBI total for the 1930 season. Wilson's revised season total of 191 RBIs remains a major league record. Although the single-season home run mark has been shattered in recent years, no one has approached Wilson's RBI record for decades. In 1979 the Veterans Committee elected Wilson to the Hall of Fame.

Who was the toughest batter to strike out?

Controversy abounds when fans argue as to who deserves the title of greatest hitter, best pitcher or finest base stealer, but there is no debate about whom the toughest player to strike out was: Cleveland Indians shortstop Joe Sewell. Sewell's career began in 1920 under unfortunate circumstances. He was the replacement for Ray Chapman, who had been killed by a Carl Mays pitch on August 16.

Sewell batted .329 in September as the Indians went on to win the American League pennant and 1920 World Series. He became the Indians regular second baseman the following season. Sewell struck out only four times in 1925 and again in 1929. After being released from the Indians in 1931, he signed with the New York Yankees. His keen eye and bat control continued as he struck out only three times in 503 at-bats for the New York Yankees in 1932. Sewell's numbers are all the more impressive if you consider that many batters have struck out five times in one game.

In 1970 San Francisco Giants outfielder Bobby Bonds set a single-season major league record with 189 strikeouts. By contrast, Sewell struck out only 113 times in his 14-year career, averaging one strikeout approximately every 62 at-bats. No other batter is remotely close to that ratio, thereby solidifying his reputation as the toughest batter to strike out in baseball history. Sewell retired with a .312 career average in 1933, and was elected by the Veterans Committee to the Hall of Fame in 1977.

Who holds the major league record for base hits in a season?

Major league records may last for days, months, or years, but special attention need be paid to any mark that remains on the books for decades. St. Louis Browns first baseman George Sisler banged out 257 hits in 1920, setting a record that lasted more than 80 years. Sisler came up to the big leagues in 1915 as a first baseman, outfielder, and pitcher. Although he showed considerable promise as a hurler, his future was as an everyday player. Sisler became one of the great hitters in the game. He had a career average of .340 and was one of only three players in the modern era with two .400 seasons. Sisler was inducted into the Hall of Fame in 1939.

Sisler no longer holds the record. In 2004, Seattle Mariners sensation Ichiro Suzuki stroked 262 hits to establish a new major league record.

⚾ ⚾ ⚾

Who holds the major league record for consecutive hits?

Nine players hold the National League record of 10 consecutive hits, but Detroit Tigers first baseman Walt Dropo set the major league mark in 1952. Dropo stroked 12 consecutive hits in 12 consecutive at-bats, and he managed to do it in only two days. "Moose" started his streak on July 14, going 5–5 against the New York Yankees. Dropo continued his hot hitting the following day as he went 4-for-4 against the Washington Senators in the opener of a doubleheader. But he wasn't done yet, stroking three hits in his first three at-bats in the second game of the twin bill.

Dropo's 12 consecutive hits tied a record set by Boston Red Sox third baseman Mike "Pinky" Higgins, who had 12 hits in 12 consecutive official at-bats during the 1938 season. Higgins walked twice during his streak. Dropo's streak of 12 consecutive hits without a base on balls established a record that has stood for more than half a century.

⚾ ⚾ ⚾

Who holds the major league record for total bases in a game?

Los Angeles Dodgers right fielder Shawn Green had a poor start to the 2002 season and was benched in the middle of a horrendous slump. Green returned to the lineup on May 23 despite a .231 average with only three homers, but his slump was about to come to a dramatic end. Green connected on a three-run homer in the second inning, and solo home runs in the fourth and fifth innings against Milwaukee Brewers pitchers. He added a single and double before homering in the ninth inning. Green went 6-for-6, slamming four home runs, a double, and a single, setting a major league mark of 19 total bases in one game.

Green broke the record set by Milwaukee Braves slugger Joe Adcock who, while using a borrowed bat, hit four homers and a double against the Brooklyn Dodgers on July 31, 1954. Adcock's 18 total bases surpassed the record of 16 set by Boston Beaneaters second baseman Bobby "Link" Lowe. Lowe hit four consecutive home runs off Cincinnati Reds right-hander Elton "Iceberg" Chamberlain on May 30, 1894. The major league record for most total bases in a game has been broken only twice in more than a century.

⚾ ⚾ ⚾

Who holds the major league record for games played in a regular season?

Each team was scheduled to play 154 games throughout much of baseball history. In 1961 the season was extended to 162 games. In 1962 Los Angeles Dodgers shortstop Maury Wills managed to play in a major league record of 165 games. How did he do it? The Dodgers ended the regular season tied with the San Francisco Giants, and a best-of-three playoff series followed to determine the National League Champions. The Giants won the playoff series 2–1, and statistics for playoff games count toward regular-season statistics.

Wills was the only player on either team who played the entire 165 games. He also stole 104 bases, breaking Ty Cobb's 47-year-old record. Wills's special season did not go unrewarded—he was named NL MVP.

Batting Awards and Titles

Who led the American League in hitting without winning the batting title?

The 1910 American League batting championship between Ty Cobb of the Detroit Tigers and Napoleon "Nap" Lajoie of the Cleveland Naps went down to the wire. Players and fans alike rooted for Lajoie to defeat his unpopular rival, but Cobb had a clear lead as they entered the final day of the season. The Naps visited the St. Louis Browns for a season-ending doubleheader, and Browns manager Jack O'Conner ordered his third baseman to play well behind the bag against Lajoie. As a result, Lajoie "beat out" six bunt singles. He also was credited with a "misplayed" triple. Lajoie edged out Cobb .384 to .383 and it appeared that the Naps second baseman secured the batting title.

But the matter wasn't settled yet. Hugh Fullerton, a sportswriter and official scorer, interceded on Cobb's behalf. Fullerton reversed a call he made on a ball that Cobb hit earlier in the season, changing his original ruling of an error to a base hit. Cobb's average jumped to .385, so Cobb edged out Lajoie for his fourth of what would be nine consecutive AL batting titles. Or did he?

Approximately 70 years later, an error was discovered that had been made in Cobb's favor. It was learned that a game in which Cobb went 2-for-3 mistakenly had been entered twice. If the error is corrected, then Cobb ended the season with a .383 average and Lajoie won the

AL title. Not so fast. The Baseball Encyclopedia and Total Baseball credit Lajoie with the higher average, but list Cobb as the 1910 AL batting champion. You figure it out.

Which American League player won the National League batting title?

A minimum number of at-bats is required to qualify for a batting title. Any player who has reached that minimum as a member of a team in one league could be traded to a team in the opposing league. Despite the trade, the player could win the batting championship with his original team. That's exactly what happened to St. Louis Cardinals outfielder Willie McGee.

McGee started the 1990 season with the Cardinals, but he was an impending free agent and became dispensable. On August 29 McGee was traded from his last-place NL team to the first-place Oakland Athletics of the American League. He had 501 at-bats and a .335 average for the Cardinals at the time of his trade. McGee played the remainder of the regular season as well as the postseason with his AL team, but he had enough at-bats to qualify for and win the NL batting title.

How close did Ted Williams come to winning the Triple Crown in 1949?

A batter must lead the league in home runs, runs batted in, and batting average in the same season in order to win the Triple Crown. Only 11 players in the modern era have accomplished this feat, and Ted Williams was one of only two hitters who twice won a Triple Crown. The "Splendid Splinter" won the Triple Crown in 1942, again in 1947, and was poised to do it once more as the 1949 season was coming to a close.

Williams had a clear lead in homers and RBIs, but he was in a battle for the hitting championship with Detroit Tigers third basemen George Kell. Williams maintained a slight edge over Kell as they entered the final day of the '49 season. But the Red Sox slugger was hitless in two official at-bats in his last game, while his rival went 2-for-3. Kell finished the season at .3429, and edged out Williams who batted .3427. Williams lost the batting title and a third Triple Crown by two thousandths of a point.

How many player/managers have won a most valuable player award?

Three different most valuable player awards have been presented since 1911. From 1911 to 14 the league's best player was honored with the Chalmers Award. It was named after an automobile company that gave a new Chalmers "30" roadster to the recipient of the award.

But controversy abounded regarding the selection process and it was discontinued in 1915. The second most valuable player award was called the League Award. It was offered from 1922 to 1929 but was discontinued for lack of interest. Beginning in 1931, the current award, called the Baseball Writers Most Valuable Player Award or simply MVP, is voted on and presented annually by the Baseball Writer's Association of America.

Although rare today, player/managers were common in the early years of baseball. Some of the more notable player/managers were the legendary Ty Cobb, Frankie "The Fordham Flash" Frisch, and baseball's all-time hit leader Pete Rose. In 1925 Cardinals second basemen Rogers Hornsby became the first player/manager to win a most valuable player award. Branch Rickey started the season as manager of the Cardinals, but he was replaced on May 30 by Hornsby between games of a day/night doubleheader. Hornsby won the Triple Crown that season as he batted .403, hit 39 home runs and drove in 143 runs. His outstanding season earned him the League Award.

The next player/manger to win a most valuable player award was catcher Mickey Cochrane. Although Cochrane played most of his career with the Philadelphia Athletics, he won the 1934 MVP in his first season with the Detroit Tigers. The last player/manager to win the MVP was Lou Boudreau, who took home the coveted award as he led the Cleveland Indians to the 1948 World Series Championship.

Who were the only players to share a Most Valuable Player Award?

It's unlikely that any vote for the Most Valuable Player Award should end in a tie, but that's exactly what happened in 1979. A couple of first basemen had outstanding seasons. Future Hall of Famer Willie Stargell led the Pittsburgh Pirates to a National League pennant and subsequent World Series Championship. "Pop" smacked 32 homers and drove in 82 runs.

Keith Hernandez of the St. Louis Cardinals also had a superb season, leading the NL in three categories having batted .344 with 48 doubles and 116 runs scored. Hernandez also was the best defensive first baseman of his day, winning 11 consecutive Gold Gloves from 1978 to 1988. Stargell and Hernandez became the only players in major league history to have tied for the Most Valuable Player Award.

⚾ ⚾ ⚾

How many players have won Rookie of the Year, Most Valuable Player, and a Gold Glove in the same season?

Rookie outfielder Fred Lynn of the Boston Red Sox batted .331 with 21 homers and 105 RBIs in 1975. He also led the American League in runs scored, doubles, and slugging percentage. Lynn was voted American League Rookie of the Year award and became the first player to also win an MVP in the same season. His spectacular season included a Gold Glove, and he became the only player to win all three awards in the same season. Lynn went on to have an impressive career, but injuries prevented him from achieving Hall of Fame stature.

Japanese sensation Ichiro Suzuki made his major league debut with the Seattle Mariners in 2001. The Mariners leadoff batter set a major league record for rookies with 242 hits as he batted .350, scored 127 runs, and had a league-leading 52 stolen bases. Suzuki was the unanimous choice for AL Rookie of the Year. He also won the MVP and a Gold Glove. Lynn and Suzuki are the only players to win all three awards in the same season.

Boston Red Sox pitcher Babe Ruth was the best left-hander in the American League before his sale in 1919 to the New York Yankees. In 1916, Ruth won 23 games for the Red Sox and led the league with nine shutouts and a 1.75 ERA. He won 24 games the following season en route to a 94–46 career record.
(National Baseball Hall of Fame Library, Cooperstown, NY)

Chapter Two

Here Comes the Pitch

"A surge of joy flooded over me that I shall never forget. I felt like shouting out that I had made a ball curve. I wanted to tell everybody—it was too good to keep to myself."
—Candy Cummings, (Pitcher for the Hartford Dark Blues and Cincinnati Red Stockings, 1876 to 1877, who has been credited with having invented the curveball.)

Perfect Games

In which game did only one player reach base?

On September 9, 1965, Los Angeles Dodgers ace Sandy Koufax faced southpaw Bob Hendley and the visiting Chicago Cubs. Both pitchers were on the top of their games. Koufax and Hendley were perfect through four innings, but in the top of the fifth inning Hendley surrendered a base on balls to Dodgers left fielder Lou Johnson. A sacrifice bunt moved Johnson to second base, and he eventually scored the only run of the game after a steal of third and a wild throw by Cubs catcher Chris Krug.

Both Koufax and Hendley continued to throw no-hit ball through six innings. Johnson would again be the spoiler as be broke up Hendley's no-hitter with a seventh-inning single. It turned out to be the only hit of the game. No other Dodger reached base. No Cub ever reached base in the contest. The Dodgers prevailed 1–0 as Koufax completed his fourth no-hitter and first perfect game.

The Dodgers officially were credited with having two base runners in the contest, but Johnson was the one and only player to reach base. Major league records were set in the game for fewest players to reach base, fewest base runners, and fewest hits. Koufax and Hendley combined to toss what may be the best pitched game in baseball history.

Who tossed a perfect game in which a runner was thrown out stealing?

A perfect game implies that no batter reached base. If no batter reached base, then how could a runner get caught stealing? Consider the following: the Boston Red Sox were scheduled to play a doubleheader against the Washington Senators on June 23, 1917. In the bottom of the first inning of the opener, the Red Sox starter screamed at umpire Brick Owens after each and every pitch. After walking leadoff batter Ray Morgan on four pitches, the pitcher rushed toward home plate in a tirade and was ejected from the game by Owens. To make matters worse, the irate pitcher punched Owens in the jaw.

Right-hander Ernie Shore came in from the bullpen, and on his first pitch, Morgan was caught stealing. Shore proceeded to retire the remaining 26 batters in a row. Was it a perfect game? It was credited as such at the time, but not anymore given revised criteria established by Major League Baseball in 1991. So it was a perfect game for more than seven decades but is now officially recorded as a combined no-hitter.

Who was the starting pitcher for the Red Sox that day? It was none other than Babe Ruth. The "Bambino" was a superb pitcher early in his career, but on this day he didn't make it past the first batter.

⚾ ⚾ ⚾

Who threw 12 perfect innings but lost?

On the evening of May 26, 1959, Pittsburgh Pirates southpaw Harvey Haddix faced right-hander Lew Burdette and the power-filled lineup of the Milwaukee Braves. But on this day, the pitchers prevailed. Haddix and Burdette threw shutout ball through 12 innings— and Haddix hadn't allowed a single runner to reach base. Burdette held the Pirates scoreless in the top of the 13th as he continued to throw shutout ball despite surrendering 12 hits in the game.

The bottom of the 13th would not be kind to Haddix. He lost his perfect game when Felix Mantilla reached first base on an error. Eddie Matthews then sacrificed Mantilla to second base. The next batter, home run king Hank Aaron, was intentionally walked. Slugger Joe Adcock came to bat and apparently slammed a home run. But Aaron left the field thinking that Adcock's hit stayed in the ballpark. Adcock then passed Aaron on the bases, and was ruled out as Mantilla scored the winning run.

Burdette registered a 2–0 shutout victory that was changed the next day to 1–0 by National League president Warren Giles. Giles ruled that both Aaron and Adcock should have been called out, and only Mantilla's run counted. It was little consolation to Haddix. In a further twist, Haddix originally was credited with a perfect game, but not any more given new rules established by Major League Baseball in 1991. He is now credited with a one-hitter rather than an "official" perfect game. Nonetheless, Pirates pitcher Bob Friend said it best when he proudly stated, "We're happy to be teammates of a man who pitched the greatest game in history."

⚾ ⚾ ⚾

Who was the only pitcher, other than Harvey Haddix, to take a perfect game into extra innings?

Harvey Haddix's 12 perfect innings are part of baseball lore, but another pitcher took a perfect game into extra innings. A couple of right-handers, Pedro Martinez of the Montreal Expos and Joey Hamilton of the San Diego Padres, faced off on June 3, 1995. Each tossed shutout ball through nine innings. Martinez, though, did not allow a single runner to reach base, becoming only the second hurler in baseball history to take a perfect game into extra innings. The Expos broke the scoreless tie with a run in the top of the 10th. Padres second baseman Bif Roberts led off the bottom of the inning with a double and ruined Martinez's chance at baseball immortality. Right hander Mel Rojas replaced Martinez and preserved a 1–0 victory. Martinez is not credited with either a no-hitter or a perfect game.

Who pitched the only perfect game in the World Series?

The Brooklyn Dodgers faced the cross-town New York Yankees in the 1956 World Series. It was the sixth time in 10 years that the teams squared off in the Fall Classic, and the "Bronx Bombers" were looking to rebound after losing to their rivals in the '55 Series. The Dodgers won the opener behind home runs by Jackie Robinson and Gil Hodges. It looked as if the Series would be tied after Game Two as the Yankees took a 6–0 lead after an inning and –a half, but Yankees starter Don Larsen was ineffective, giving up four runs in one and two thirds innings. The Dodgers rallied to win the contest, taking a two-game Series lead. Despite the disappointing loss, the Yankees bounced back to win Games Three and Four.

Right-hander Sal Maglie started Game Five for the Dodgers. Yankees manager Casey Stengel decided to start Larsen despite his earlier shellacking. Larsen rewarded his manager's confidence in him, retiring the first 24 Dodgers. The Yankees had a 2–0 lead as the Dodgers came to bat in the top of the ninth. Larsen needed three more outs. Carl Furillo led off the inning and fouled off four pitches before Larsen got him to hit a routine fly ball to right field for the first out. As the tension grew, Dodgers catcher Roy Campanella hit an easy ground ball to second baseman Billy Martin for the second out. The next batter Larsen faced was pinch-hitter Dale Mitchell. With the crowd in a near frenzy and the count at 2-and-2, Mitchell struck out on a called third strike by umpire Babe Pinelli. Larsen had his perfect game.

The Yankees won the '56 Series in seven games.

No-hitters

Was there ever a double no-hitter?

On May 2, 1917, the visiting Cincinnati Reds started nine right-handed batters against Chicago Cubs southpaw Hippo Vaughn. But the strategy failed to generate any offense as Vaughan gave up no runs or hits through nine innings. Reds right-hander Fred Toney didn't have to face nine left-handed hitters, but he too had a no-hit shutout going through nine innings. It was the only time in baseball history that opposing pitchers both threw a nine-inning no-hitter in the same game.

In the top of the 10th inning, Reds shortstop Larry Kopf lined a one-out single to break up Vaughn's no-hitter. One out later Cubs center fielder Cy Williams dropped Hal Chase's line drive for an error as Kopf went to third base on the play. The next batter, legendary athlete Jim Thorpe, hit a slow grounder to Vaughn, who threw home but failed to prevent Kopf from scoring the go-ahead run. Toney retired the Cubs in the bottom of the 10th without allowing a hit and the Reds escaped with a 1–0 victory.

Both pitchers originally were credited with a no-hitter, but Major League Baseball enacted new rules in 1991, and now only Toney is credited with an "official" no-hitter. Nonetheless, it was a game for the ages.

⚾ ⚾ ⚾

Who threw a no-hitter in his first major league start?

St. Louis Browns right-hander Bobo Holloman didn't waste any time for his chance at baseball immortality. Although Holloman had been ineffective in four games as a reliever, Browns manager Marty Marion chose him as the starting pitcher against the Philadelphia Athletics on May 6, 1953. Marion's confidence was rewarded as Holloman tossed a no-hitter, becoming the only pitcher in the modern era to have achieved that feat in his first big league start. The no-hitter turned out to be Holloman's only shutout, only complete game, and one of only three wins in his only season of major league baseball.

Holloman also contributed at the plate that memorable day with two singles and three RBIs, which happened to be the only hits and only RBIs of his career.

Which one-armed pitcher tossed a no-hitter?

Despite being born without a right arm, southpaw Jim Abbott excelled in both the collegiate and professional ranks. In 1989 Abbott went directly from the University of Michigan to the California Angels. Whenever on the mound, Abbott placed a right-handed glove against the stump of his right arm. Immediately after delivering a pitch, Abbott switched the glove to his left hand for defensive purposes. He won 87 games in his career, but none more memorable than the one on September 4, 1993. Playing for the New York Yankees in the heat of a pennant race, Abbott tossed a no-hitter against the visiting Cleveland Indians. It was the highlight of a major league career that lasted 10 years.

Abbott is not the only one-handed player to make it to the big leagues. Pete Gray lost an arm in a childhood accident but managed to reach the big leagues. Gray was a natural right-hander who taught himself to throw and bat from the left side. He had an impressive minor league career, including a .333 average with five homers for the Memphis Chicks of the Southern Association in 1944. Gray's outstanding play earned him a spot on the St. Louis Browns in 1945. Surprisingly, his teammates were less than supportive as they rode him mercilessly about his disability. Gray was demoted when major league players, who had been serving in World War II, returned to the diamond.

🟡 🟡 🟡

Who pitched a no-hitter against his brother?

No-hitters have been thrown. Brothers have squared off against each other. But only once has a pitcher tossed a no-hitter with his brother on the opposing team. Cleveland Indians right-hander Wes Ferrell threw a no-hitter against his older brother Rick and the St. Louis Browns on April 29, 1931. Wes contributed to his cause that day with a homer, double, and four RBIs. He was one of the best hitting pitchers in the game. Wes hit nine round-trippers in 1931, setting a major league record for homers in a season by a pitcher. He went on to set another major league record for pitchers, hitting 38 career home runs.

Wes also had an impressive career on the mound. He was a six-time 20-game winner, and recorded 193 career victories. Wes and Rick played together for the Boston Red Sox from 1934 to 1937, and both were traded to the Washington Senators during the '37 season. They often worked together as battery-mates until Wes retired in 1941. Although Wes was a pitcher, he had more career home runs than his brother. On the other hand,

Rick was a superb defensive catcher, and batted at or near .300 for seven consecutive seasons from 1931 to 1937. Rick was elected by the Veterans Committee to the Hall of Fame in 1984.

⚾ ⚾ ⚾

Who threw two consecutive no-hitters?

Cincinnati Reds southpaw Johnny Vander Meer faced the visiting Boston Bees on June 11, 1938. Vander Meer, who was in the first full season of his major league career, threw a no-hitter against the Bees. At that time, only two pitchers in baseball history had recorded two career no-hitters, and no one had thrown two no-hitters in the same season—let alone in consecutive games. Vander Meer's next start was on June 15 when he faced the Brooklyn Dodgers in the first night game ever played at Ebbets Field.

Although Vander Meer was erratic throughout the contest, he managed to keep the Dodgers hitless through eight innings. He retired the leadoff hitter in the bottom of the ninth inning, but walked the next three batters. Vander Meer then got a force out at home plate for the second out of the inning. With two out and the bases loaded, player/manager Leo Durocher hit a short pop fly for the final out. Before more than 40,000 avid fans, Vander Meer tossed his second consecutive no-hitter. No hurler has matched Vander Meer's accomplishment.

Who threw a no-hitter in each of four consecutive seasons?

Few pitchers have thrown two or more no-hitters. Some of them have done so in consecutive seasons, but only one hurler has tossed a no-hitter in each of four consecutive seasons. An educated guess might lead one to think it was Nolan Ryan, but it was Dodgers southpaw Sandy Koufax. Although Koufax began his major league carrier with the Brooklyn Dodgers, his most productive years were with the Los Angeles Dodgers. In 1962 Koufax threw the first of his no-hitters against the fledgling New York Mets. The following season the Dodgers' ace tossed his second no-hitter. In 1964 Koufax no-hit the Philadelphia Phillies, but the best was yet to come. On September 9, 1965, he threw a perfect game and his fourth no-hitter, defeating the Chicago Cubs and a near-perfect Bob Hendley.

Koufax is one of the greatest hurlers in the game. He won the Cy Young Award in 1963, 1965 and 1966—an especially impressive feat at the time given that only one pitcher in all of baseball was awarded the coveted honor. Koufax may have had his best season in 1963 when he went 25–5 with a 1.88 ERA and 306 strikeouts, leading the National League in victories, ERA, shutouts, and strikeouts. His performance was so dominating it also earned him the NL MVP, but he wasn't done yet. Koufax led the Dodgers to a World Series sweep of the New York Yankees and was voted World Series MVP.

Koufax continued his mastery over NL batters through the 1966 season when he went 27–9, leading the league in victories, ERA, strikeouts, shutouts, innings pitched, games started and complete games. For the second straight year, Koufax was the unanimous winner of the Cy Young Award. But the great left-hander would retire from the game at season's end due to persistent arm problems. In 1972 Koufax became the youngest player inducted into the Hall of Fame.

⚾ ⚾ ⚾

What were the most runs given up in a no-hitter?

Pitchers occasionally have given up one or two runs in the course of tossing a no-hitter, but New York Yankees right-hander Andy Hawkins did even better (or worse). On July 1, 1990, Hawkins held the Chicago White Sox hitless through seven innings and retired the first two batters in the bottom of the eighth when Yankees third baseman Mike Blowers booted Sammy Sosa's ground ball for an error. Sosa stole second, and Hawkins walked Ozzie Guillen and Lance Johnson to load the bases. The next batter, Robin Ventura, hit a fly ball to left field that was misplayed for an error by rookie Jim Leyritz. Sosa, Guillen, and Johnson all scored as Ventura took second base. Ivan Calderon followed with a high fly to right fielder Jesse Barfield, who lost the ball in the sun for yet another error, allowing Ventura to score the fourth run of the inning.

The Yankees were retired in the top of the ninth inning as the White Sox secured a victory without the benefit of a base hit. Despite surrendering four runs, Hawkins threw a complete game no-hitter that went the distance. Although he was credited with a no-hitter at the time, Major League Baseball enacted new rules in 1991 that prevent Hawkins's performance from being classified as an "official" no-hitter. Perhaps those rules should be revisited.

What were the most pitchers involved in a combined no-hitter?

On June 11, 2003, the Houston Astros visited Yankee Stadium to play an inter-league game with the Bronx Bombers. Roy Oswalt started for the Astros but left the game in the second inning with a groin injury. Manger Jimmy Williams brought in Pete Munro, who tossed two and two thirds hitless innings. Kirk Saarloos followed with one and one third innings of hitless relief. Brad Lidge, who was credited with the victory, kept the no-hitter intact through seven innings. Octavio Dotel held the Yankees hitless in the eighth inning, striking out four batters as one batter reached base on a passed ball after striking out. Closer Bill Wagner retired the side in order in the ninth inning, completing the six-pitcher no-hitter.

Who lost three no-hitters, each with two out in the ninth inning?

Losing a no-hitter with two out in the ninth inning must count as one of the most frustrating moments for a pitcher. Toronto Blue Jays right-hander Dave Stieb had good reason to be deeply frustrated in 1988 and 1989. On September 24, 1988, Stieb held the Cleveland Indians hitless until the bottom of the ninth inning with two out when Julio Franco got a bad-hop single over the head of the Blue Jays second baseman Manuel Lee. The Blue Jays prevailed 1–0 despite the unlucky bounce, but Stieb lost his no-hitter.

In his next and last start of the season on September 30, Stieb again was one out away from a no-hitter when Baltimore Orioles pinch-hitter Jim Traber hit a bloop single over the head of the Blue Jays first basemen. Once again, Stieb was heartbreakingly close to baseball immortality. His third near miss occurred on August 4, 1989. Stieb had a perfect game ruined when New York Yankees center fielder Roberto Kelly doubled with two out in the ninth inning. In less than a year, the hard luck pitcher lost three no-hitters with two out in the ninth inning.

Stieb flirted with no-hitters on other occasions. In 1989 alone, he tossed two additional one-hitters. On April 10 Yankees catcher Jamie Quirk's fifth inning single broke up Stieb's no-hitter. It was Stieb's third one-hitter in his last four starts dating back to the 1988 season. On August 26 of the '89 season, Stieb threw another one-hitter. Milwaukee Brewers All-Star Robin Yount spoiled that pitching gem with a sixth-inning single.

At long last, Stieb tossed a no-hitter against the Cleveland Indians on September 2, 1990. It was the first no-hitter in the history of the Blue Jays' franchise.

⚾ ⚾ ⚾

What was unusual about Virgil Trucks's 1952 season?

Right-hander Virgil "Fire" Trucks begin his major league career with the Detroit Tigers in 1941. He was an effective pitcher for the Tigers throughout the early part of his career. Trucks won more than a hundred games prior to 1952 despite missing nearly three full seasons. He didn't play in 1944 and played only one regular season game in 1945, having served his country in World War II. Trucks also missed almost the entire 1950 season due to an injury. Nevertheless, he won 14 or more games for the Tigers on five occasions, including a 19-victory season in 1949 when he led the league in strikeouts and tied for the lead in shutouts.

After registering a 13–8 record for the Tigers in 1951, Trucks seemed primed for the '52 season. Although he pitched effectively that year, including a lower ERA than the prior season, Trucks went a dismal 5–19 with the anemic hitting Tigers. But the season had its high points. On May 15, 1952, Trucks tossed a 1–0 no-hitter against the Washington Senators. A home run by slugger Vic

Wertz with two out in the bottom of the ninth inning sealed the victory and preserved the no-hitter. On August 25 he tossed his second no-hitter of the season, defeating the New York Yankees, also by a score of 1–0.

The no-hitter against the Yankees was in doubt for a few innings. A ball hit by Phil Rizzuto was bobbled by Tigers shortstop Johnny Pesky and the official scorer ruled it an error. He later changed his ruling to a hit. At the end of the sixth inning, the official scorer again ruled it an error. That decision preserved Trucks' second no-hitter of the season—not bad for a 5–19 season.

Pitching Records

Which American League ERA leader pitched only on Sundays?

Right-hander Ted Lyons played his entire 21-year career with the Chicago White Sox. Despite playing for a perennial second-division team, Lyons led American League pitchers in victories in 1925 and again in 1927. He developed a knuckleball later in his career to compensate for an injured shoulder, and continued to win regularly for the hapless White Sox. Beginning in 1939, White Sox manager Jimmie Dykes decided to pitch the 38-year-old Lyons mostly on Sunday afternoons in order to preserve his arm and draw large crowds that came to see the popular pitcher.

Lyons' popularity reached a peak on September 15, 1940 when Chicago fans celebrated Ted Lyons Day. Lyons rewarded his adoring fans by winning the opener of a doubleheader against the Boston Red Sox. Dykes continued to pitch Lyons almost exclusively on Sundays over the next few seasons. In 1942 "Sunday Teddy" started and completed every one of his 20 games. Nearly all of those 20 games were, of course, on Sunday. Lyons finished the season with a 14–6 record and an AL-leading ERA of 2.10. The beloved White Sox pitcher retired from the game with 260 career victories, an impressive number given that he played his entire career with one of the weakest teams in the league. Lyons was inducted into the Hall of Fame in 1955.

⚾ ⚾ ⚾

How many pitchers tossed complete-game shutouts in both ends of a doubleheader?

Although it was not at all unusual for pitchers to throw both ends of a doubleheader in the early years of baseball, it was noteworthy if the hurler tossed a couple of shutouts. It happened in the midst of the 1908 National League pennant race between the Chicago Cubs, Pittsburgh Pirates, and New York Giants. The teams were in a virtual three-way tie at the beginning of play on September 26 when the Cubs visited Ebbets Field to play a doubleheader against the Brooklyn Dodgers. Cubs right-hander Ed Reulbach tossed a five-hit 5–0 shutout in the opener. A tired Cubs pitching staff forced manager Frank Chance to start Reulbach in the second end of the twin bill. "Big Ed" responded with a three-hit 3–0 shutout. Reulbach is the only pitcher in baseball history to throw complete-game shutouts in both ends of a doubleheader.

Who has the major league record for complete-game victories in both ends of a doubleheader?

Only 11 pitchers in the modern era have registered complete-game victories in both ends of a doubleheader, and one of them did it on three separate occasions. Although New York Yankees great Lou Gehrig was known as the "Iron Horse," right-hander Joe McGinnity was the "Iron Man" of the New York Giants pitching staff from 1902 to 1908. McGinnity had the nickname prior to his big league career as a result of working in a family-owned iron foundry, but he more than earned that moniker throughout his major league career.

McGinnity teamed with the legendary Christy Mathewson to form one of the most fearsome pitching duos in the history of the game. McGinnity and Mathewson each won 30 games in 1903 and again in 1904. In 1903 the "Iron Man" led the league in games started, games completed, and innings pitched—tossing 434 innings. McGinnity also led the National League in games pitched from 1903 to 1907.

It was not at all uncommon for McGinnity to pitch both ends of a doubleheader, and he is the only pitcher in baseball history to win both ends of a doubleheader three times. It did not take an entire career to accomplish that feat. It didn't even take a season. McGinnity managed to win the three doubleheaders in one month. His first two twin bill sweeps came in the first week of August during the 1903 season, and he added one more doubleheader sweep at the end of the month.

McGinnity was elected by the Veterans Committee to the Hall of Fame in 1946.

Which team had the most pitchers with ERAs below 2.00 in a season?

Few pitchers today give up less than two earned runs a game for the season. It's happened on only 10 occasions in the last three decades. Since 1973 the entire American League has had a mere three pitchers who have had ERAs below 2.00. But low ERAs were the norm during the Deadball Era (1901 to 1919). Eighteen major league pitchers had sub-2.00 ERAs in 1908 and again in 1909. Not only did hurlers regularly record ERAs below 2.00, but many approached 1.00 and Boston Red Sox southpaw Dutch Leonard established a major league mark as he recorded a microscopic ERA of .961 in 1914.

Entire pitching staffs recorded low ERAs during the Deadball Era. The Chicago Cubs pitching staff alone had a team ERA below 2.00 in 1905, 1906, 1907 and 1909.

The 1906 Cubs pitching staff as well as the 1909 Philadelphia Athletics each had four starters giving up less than two earned runs a game for the season, but it was the 1907 Cubs who had each of their five starters with an ERA below 2.00. They were Jack Pfiester, Carl Lundgren, Mordecai "Three-Finger" Brown, Orval Overall and "Big Ed" Reulbach. Pfiester led the league with a 1.15 ERA, barely edging out Lundgren who recorded a 1.17 ERA.

Unless substantive changes are made in the game, no other pitching staff will have five starters who give up less than two earned runs per game in one season.

Which pitcher won the most games in a season?

The New York Highlanders were a half game behind the league-leading Boston Pilgrims on the final day of the 1904 season. A doubleheader was scheduled between the teams and the Highlanders needed to sweep both ends of the twin bill in order to capture the American League pennant. Highlanders right-hander Jack Chesbro, who had a record of 41–11, started the opener. The score was tied 2–2 in the top of the ninth inning with two out and a runner on third base. Chesbro, who was known to throw the spit ball, then unleashed a wet and wild pitch over the head of his catcher that allowed the go-ahead run to score. In the bottom of the ninth, right-hander Bill Dinnenn retired the side as the Pilgrims won the AL pennant.

Despite a disappointing end to the season, Chesbro established a major league record with 41 victories in a season. His record stands today and should last into the foreseeable future since no pitcher has started as many as 40 games in a season for nearly two decades.

🔘 🔘 🔘

Which pitcher lost the most games in a season?

No pitcher has lost as many as 30 games in a season, but right-hander Vic Willis came perilously close. Willis was a fine pitcher who put together eight 20-win seasons for the Boston Beaneaters and Pittsburgh Pirates, but in 1905 he lost 29 games for the Beaneaters. It was not completely surprising since he was on one of the worst teams in baseball history. Each of the four starters on the team was a 20-game loser. The only other team with four 20-game losers in a season was the 1906 Beaneaters, but Willis was no longer with the team.

Willis was traded to the Pittsburgh Pirates, and proceeded to string together four consecutive 20-win seasons. He ended his career with 249 victories. Despite setting a major league record for most losses in a season, Willis was elected by the Veterans Committee to the Hall of Fame in 1995.

🔘 🔘 🔘

Which pitcher holds the major league record for consecutive wins?

New York Giants left-hander Carl Hubbell was one of the great pitchers in the history of baseball. His trademark knuckleball baffled National League hitters for more than a decade, and he was at the very top of his game during the 1936 and 1937 seasons. "The Meal Ticket" won his last 16 decisions in 1936 and his first eight decisions in 1937, setting a major league record with 24 consecutive victories. Hubbell's performance during the '36 season was particularly impressive as he led the league in victories and ERA—helping to earn him his second Most Valuable Player Award.

Hubbell's accomplishments are the stuff of legends, including election to the Hall of Fame in 1947, but he will best be known for his startling performance in the 1935 All-Star Game. Hubbell started for the National League in major league baseball's second All Star Game. He got off to a rocky start, giving up a single and base on balls to begin the contest, but Hubbell proceeded to strike out Babe Ruth, Lou Gehrig, and Jimmy Foxx to end the inning. A home run in the bottom of the first by Frankie Frisch gave the NL squad a 1–0 lead.

Hubbell began the second inning by striking out Al Simmons and Joe Cronin, before giving up a single and then striking out Lefty Gomez to end the inning. "King Carl" consecutively fanned five future Hall of Famers.

⚾ ⚾ ⚾

Which pitcher holds the major league record for consecutive losses?

Anthony Young, a promising young right-hander for the New York Mets, began the 1992 season with two victories. Although he had a measure of success as a starter, manager Jeff Torborg moved Young to the bullpen where he pitched effectively. Young picked up save after save as he tossed 23 $\frac{2}{3}$ consecutive shutout innings, but victories were elusive. Despite racking up 15 saves for the season, Young lost his last 14 decisions.

The following season would begin in much the same way that the '92 season ended. Young continued to lose one game after another. One month into the season, Dallas Green replaced Torborg as manager. Green later put Young back into the starting rotation, but to no avail. Young lost all of his five starts in June and went down to his 27th consecutive defeat on July 24.

It appeared that Young would lose again on July 28 when he gave up the go-ahead run in the top of the ninth inning against the Florida Marlins, but the Mets rallied for two runs in the bottom of the inning to give Young his first victory in more than a year. It was a good thing since Young lost his last three decisions of the season.

⚾ ⚾ ⚾

Which pitcher holds the major league record for consecutive losses in one season?

Right-hander Jack Nabors pitched for the Philadelphia Athletics from 1915 to 1917. In his rookie season he went 0–5, but the worst was yet to come. On Opening Day of the 1916 season, Boston Red Sox left-hander Babe Ruth defeated Nabors and the Athletics 2–1. But

Nabors bounced back to beat the Red Sox, evening his season record at 1–1. That would be his last victory of the season. In fact, that would be the last victory of his career. Nabors went on to lose a major league record of 19 consecutive games in one season. His 1–20 season as well as his 1–25 career mark are records for futility that have stood the test of time.

In all fairness to Nabors, he had the misfortune of playing on an extraordinarily mediocre team. The 1916 Athletics had a dismal record of 36–117, including a 20-game losing streak. Athletics right-hander Tom Sheehan managed to do a bit better than Nabors, going 1–16 for the season. Two other members of the pitching staff had 20-loss seasons. But victories were scarce for a reason. The Athletics, by a large margin, scored the fewest runs of any team in the league. Nabors may have had the worst season on the worst team in the history of the game.

Who holds the major league record for most consecutive complete games?

Right-hander Jack Taylor put together a streak of consecutive complete games that began on June 20, 1901 and ended more than five years later on August 9, 1906. Taylor started and completed 187 games over that period, including an 18-inning and 19-inning contest. For good measure, Taylor tossed in 15 relief appearances—and he completed each of them as well.

Excluding his final season, Taylor completed 270 out of 273 games over his career. He set the single-season mark in 1904, throwing 39 consecutive complete games for the St. Louis Cardinals. By contrast, no major league pitcher in this century has thrown as many as 10 complete games in a season. Rarely will you see a hurler throw two or three consecutive games. Taylor's mark should last for some time.

⚾ ⚾ ⚾

Which pitcher holds the major league record for consecutive no-hit innings?

Johnny Vander Meer pitched back-to-back no-hitters and set a National League record with 21 ⅔ consecutive hitless innings, but the legendary Cy Young of the Boston Pilgrims holds the major league mark. Young's streak began on April 25, 1904, when he held the Philadelphia Athletics hitless over the last two innings of the game. In his next appearance, Young threw seven no-hit innings in relief against the Washington Senators, extending his consecutive no-hit innings streak to nine innings.

Young faced his nemesis Athletics lefty Rube Waddell on May 5 and threw the first perfect game of the modern era. The intense pitcher was so focused on defeating Waddell that he didn't realize a perfect game had been thrown until his teammates ran on the field to congratulate him. Additionally, Young's no-hit streak reached 18 consecutive innings. He opened his next start with six no-hit innings against the Detroit Tigers before giving up a one-out single in the seventh. Young set a major league record of 24 ⅓ hitless innings.

What controversial call allowed Don Drysdale to set a record for consecutive shutout innings?

In 1968 Los Angeles Dodger right-hander Don Drysdale was chasing Walter Johnson's major league record of 55 ⅔ consecutive shutout innings. On May 31 Drysdale faced the San Francisco Giants, having tossed four consecutive shutouts and 36 consecutive scoreless innings. Drysdale threw shutout ball through the first eight innings before loading the bases with no out in the top of the ninth.

Drysdale's streak apparently ended when he hit Giants catcher Dick Dietz, but home plate umpire Harry Wendelstedt ruled that Dietz made no attempt to avoid the pitch and was not entitled to first base. The rulebook states that a ball is in the strike zone when "The batter makes no attempt to avoid being touched by the ball" (see rule 6.08[b] [2]). Wendelstedt's rarely enforced ruling prevented a run from scoring. Drysdale went on to retire Dietz as well as the next two batters without allowing a run, thereby preserving his consecutive scoreless innings streak.

Drysdale tossed a record-setting sixth consecutive shutout against the visiting Pittsburgh Pirates on June 4, extending his scoreless innings streak to 54 ^{2}/$_3$ innings. The big right-hander held the Philadelphia Phillies scoreless over the first four innings in his next pitching appearance, setting a major league record, one that has since been broken, with 58 ^{2}/$_3$ consecutive scoreless innings Drysdale broke Johnson's record, but it took a gutsy call from Wendelstedt to keep the streak alive.

⚾ ⚾ ⚾

Who was the last 30-game winner?

A dozen pitchers in the modern era have had 30-win seasons, but it's been almost four decades since any major league pitcher has reached that plateau. In 1968 Detroit Tigers right-hander Denny McLain went 31–6, leading his team to a World Series Championship. McLain's special season wasn't over as he became the unanimous winner of both the Cy Young Award and American League MVP. Prior to McLain, the last pitcher to have a 30-win season was St. Louis Cardinals ace Dizzy Dean, who went an impressive 30–7 in 1934. McLain is the only pitcher in the last 70 years to have a 30-win season.

On September 19 of the '68 season, McLain had a commanding 6–1 lead over the New York Yankees and was well on the way to his 31st victory. Yankees center fielder Mickey Mantle was in the last year of his stellar career and was tied for third place in career homers with Philadelphia Athletics Hall of Famer Jimmy Foxx, but the season was rapidly winding down. McLain called Tigers catcher Jim Price to the mound in the top of the eighth inning and instructed Price to let Mantle know that an easy fastball was about to sail over the plate. The Yankees slugger took the pitch in disbelief.

McClain again told Price to inform Mantle that the ball was about to be lobbed over the plate. This time an alert Mantle proceeded to hit his 535th round-tripper, passing Foxx in career home runs. As Mantle rounded third base, he tipped his hat to McClain.

⚾ ⚾ ⚾

Which players have won Rookie of the Year, Cy Young, and Most Valuable Player Awards?

Although Major League Baseball has honored a most valuable player throughout much of the modern era, the Baseball Writers Association of America first awarded in 1931 what is currently known as the MVP. A Rookie of the Year trophy was originally handed out in 1947 and the inaugural Cy Young Award was given in 1956. Brooklyn Dodgers right-hander Don Newcombe went 17–8 with a 3.17 ERA in 1949, including a league-leading five shutouts, earning him the National League Rookie of the Year Award.

"Newk" went on to be one of the top pitchers in the senior circuit. He averaged almost 20 wins a season through 1956, excluding 1952 and 1953 when he served in the military. Newcombe may have had his finest season in 1956 when he went 27–7 with a 3.06 ERA. His performance earned him the inaugural Cy Young Award as well as the NL MVP, becoming the first pitcher to win both honors in the same season and the only pitcher to win three of baseball's most coveted awards.

How many pitchers won the Rookie of the Year and Cy Young Awards in the same season?

Los Angeles Dodgers southpaw Jerry Reuss was the scheduled starter for Opening Day of the 1981 season. But an injury to Reuss forced rookie left-hander Fernando Valenzuela to take his place on the mound. In his first major league start, Valenzuela responded with a 2–0 shutout of the Houston Astros, but the best was yet to come. The popular Mexican star won his first eight games, baffling National League hitters with his trademark screwball as his eyes rolled skyward.

"Fernandomania" had taken over Southern California, but Valenzuela's phenomenal start was put on hold for two months in the middle of the season due to a players' strike. Valenzuela completed the season with a 13–7 mark and a 2.48 ERA, leading the league in shutouts, strikeouts and innings pitched. His eight shutouts tied a NL rookie record and might have more impressive were it not for the strike-shortened season. Valenzuela's performance earned him the Rookie of the Year and Cy Young Awards, becoming the first and only player to take home both trophies in the same season.

Which brothers hold the major league record for career wins?

Knuckleballer Phil Niekro played for four teams, mostly with the Atlanta Braves, in his 24-year career. He was a three-time 20-game winner and a five-time All-Star. Phil won 318 games in his career and was inducted into the Hall of Fame in 1997. His younger brother Joe played for seven teams in his 22-year career. Joe was a 20-game winner for the Houston Astros in 1979 and 1980, and won 221 games in his career. The Niekro boys won a total of 539 games, setting a standard unequalled by any other brother tandem.

In 1986, Joe was with the Astros and Phil was with the Braves. The two teams faced each other on May 29, and in the top of the seventh inning Joe hit the first and only home run of his long career. Brother Phil surrendered the homer.

Who holds the record for fewest pitches thrown in a nine-inning complete game?

Although few pitchers throw under a hundred pitches in a nine-inning complete game these days, it was far from uncommon decades ago. Many pitchers tossed complete games having thrown pitches in the 90s, 80s, 70s, or even the 60s, but Boston Braves right-hander Charles "Red" Barrett went into the 50s. Barrett was an eccentric player known for his sense of humor, but he was all business on August 10, 1944, allowing only two batters to reach base en route to a 2–0 shutout of the Cincinnati Reds. Barrett gave up two singles, and neither walked nor struck out a batter. In the process, he threw a major league low of 58 pitches in the game.

⚾ ⚾ ⚾

What were the most hits surrendered in a nine-inning shutout?

A couple of 19-game winners, Chicago Cubs right-hander Larry Cheney and New York Giants southpaw Rube Marquard, faced off on September 14, 1913. Cheney was not particularly overpowering that day—the Giants managed to hit safely in each inning, but they could not get a runner across home plate. Cheney was aided by his battery-mate, who caught three Giants base runners attempting to steal. Another Giants base runner was thrown out attempting to stretch a single into a double. Cheney benefited from the poor base running and shutout the Giants, despite surrendering 14 hits in the game.

⚾ ⚾ ⚾

What's the longest save by a relief pitcher?

Saves became part of the official record in 1969. Most saves are an inning or less. Other saves have been two or three innings, but few saves are four or more innings. Texas Rangers rookie right-hander Joaquin Benoit went well beyond that on September 3, 2002 in a game against the Baltimore Orioles. In the top of the first inning, a pitch thrown by Orioles right-hander John Stephens hit Rangers All-Star Alex Rodriguez. In the bottom of the inning, Rangers starter Aaron Myette retaliated as his first two pitches were thrown behind leadoff batter Melvin Mora. Home plate umpire Mark Hirschbeck had seen enough and ejected Myette from the game.

Right-hander Todd Van Poppel came in from the bullpen and held the Orioles scoreless in the inning. The Rangers then scored three runs in the top of the second inning. Van Poppel proceeded to toss a scoreless bottom of the second, but that would be his last inning. Benoit came in from the bullpen and effectively held the Orioles in check throughout the remainder of the game. A leadoff ninth-inning triple was the Orioles' only hit of the contest. The official scorer credited Van Poppel with the victory and Benoit with a major league record seven-inning save.

Strikeouts and Bases on Balls

How many pitchers twice struck out four batters in an inning?

It's not often that a pitcher strikes out four batters in one inning, but Anaheim Angels left-hander Chuck Finley managed to do it on May 12, 1999. Finley struck out the first two New York Yankees hitters in the third inning, but his third strikeout victim reached base on a wild pitch. Finley struck out the next batter, and tied a major league record shared by fewer than 40 pitchers. Nolan Ryan, Roger Clemens, and Randy Johnson, the all time career strikeout leaders, never struck out four batters in an inning.

But Finley was not done yet. On August 15, 1999, Finley and the Angels visited Tigers Stadium to play an afternoon against Detroit. Finley gave up a first-inning leadoff single, but struck out the following two batters. His third strikeout victim of the inning reached base on a wild pitch, but the next batter struck out to end the inning. Finley did it again. He is the only pitcher in baseball history to twice strike out four batters in an inning.

Finley became a free agent at the end of the '99 season and signed with the Cleveland Indians. Finley and his new team faced the visiting Texas Rangers on April 16, 2000. One of Finley's strikeout victims reached first base on a passed ball in the third inning, allowing the big lefty to again strike out four batters in an inning. No other pitcher in baseball history has twice struck out four batters in an inning, but Finley managed to do it three times—in less than a year.

⚾ ⚾ ⚾

Who was the first pitcher to strike out 20 batters in a nine-inning game?

Boston Red Sox right-hander Roger Clemens had his breakthrough season in 1986. Clemens went 24–4 with a 2.48 ERA, and earned both the American League Cy Young Award as well as the AL Most Valuable Player Award. There were early indications that Clemens might be primed for a special season. On April 29, 1986, he set a major league record when he struck out 20 Seattle Mariners en route to a 3–1 victory. Clemens broke the previous record of 19 strikeouts that was shared by Steve Carlton, Nolan Ryan, and Tom Seaver.

Who was the next pitcher to strike out 20 batters in a game? Ten years later on September 18, 1996, the irrepressible Clemens did it once again. He fanned 20 Detroit Tigers on the way to a 4–0 shutout. Only one other pitcher has struck out 20 batters in a nine-inning game. Chicago Cubs rookie right-hander Kerry Wood did it on May 6, 1998 against the Houston Astros.

The major league record for strikeouts in a game is held by Washington Senators right-hander Tom Cheney. On September 12, 1962, Cheney struck out 21 Baltimore Orioles—but it took him 16 innings.

⚾ ⚾ ⚾

Who holds the record for strikeouts by a pitcher in a major league debut?

Brooklyn Dodgers southpaw Karl Spooner had an impressive start to his baseball career. Spooner burst into the big leagues on September 22, 1954, shutting out the pennant-winning New York Giants. He struck out 15 batters in the game, setting a major league record for strikeouts by a pitcher in a major league debut. Spooner also struck out six consecutive batters in the game, setting another major league mark for pitchers making their first big league start.

Spooner followed his outstanding debut with a 12-strikeout 1–0 shutout of the Pittsburgh Pirates that featured Gil Hodges' 42nd homer. Spooner set another major league record, striking out 27 batters in his first two starts. His future in baseball looked bright. Unfortunately, he injured his arm the following year during spring training. Although Spooner pitched effectively during the 1955 season, he never fully recovered from the injury and made his final appearance in Game Six of the '55 World Series.

The Dodgers defeated the New York Yankees in Game Seven to win their first and only World Series Championship. Spooner had an abbreviated career, but at least he took home a World Series ring.

⚾ ⚾ ⚾

Who holds the record for consecutive strike-outs?

It's noteworthy anytime a pitcher chalks up strike-out after strikeout. A handful of pitchers have managed to strike out eight batters in a row, but only one has reached double digits. On April 22, 1970, New York Mets ace right-hander Tom Seaver had an amazing afternoon. Prior to the game, Seaver accepted his Cy Young

Award for his 1969 season in which he went 25–7 with a 2.21 ERA. Seaver also started the game with a 12-game winning streak dating back to the '69 season when he won his last 10 decisions.

Seaver continued to pitch dominant ball that day, giving credence to his nickname "The Franchise." He struck out 19 San Diego Padres to tie a major league record for a nine-inning game set one year earlier by St. Louis Cardinals lefty Steve Carlton. Their mark has since been broken by right-hander Roger Clemens who struck out 20 batters for the Boston Red Sox in 1986 and again 10 years later in 1996. In 1998 Chicago Cubs rookie right-hander Kerry Wood tied Clemens mark in only his fifth career start, striking out 20 Houston Astros.

In the game of April 22, Seaver did set a major league record that stands today as he struck out the final 10 Padres batters. No other hurler in the history of the game has fanned 10 consecutive batters.

Which 300 single-season strikeout pitcher relieved another 300 single-season strikeout pitcher?

Few pitchers have struck out 300 batters in a season. One team had two pitchers who had reached the 300-strikeout milestone, and one of them came in to relieve the other—in a game that took two days to complete. Arizona Diamondbacks right-hander Curt Schilling, a

300-strikeout pitcher for the Philadelphia Phillies in 1997 and 1998, completed two perfect innings on July 18, 2001 when an explosion in a leftfield light tower in San Diego's Qualcomm Stadium caused the game to be suspended.

When play resumed the following day, Diamondbacks southpaw Randy Johnson, who was well on his way to his fourth 300-strikeout season, relieved for Schilling. "The Big Unit" went on to strike out 16 batters in his seven-inning stint, setting a major league record for strikeouts as a reliever. Schilling and Johnson combined to allow only one hit in the contest, an eight-inning single by Wiki Gonzalez. Johnson also set a major league record for relievers as he fanned seven consecutive batters.

⚾ ⚾ ⚾

Which pitcher holds the National League record for allowing the most walks in one game?

Would any manager allow his pitcher to walk 10 or more batters in a game? New York Giants skipper John McGraw, who was better known for his impatience, did exactly that in the final game of the 1906 season. McGraw called on Henry Mathewson, younger brother of Hall-of-Famer Christy, to start against the last-place Boston Beaneaters. The Giants were out of the pennant race and McGraw gave Henry a chance to prove himself. Unfortunately, Henry had less than stellar control as he walked 14 Beaneaters, setting a National League record in the process. He managed to hit another batter, but did toss a complete game in defeat.

It was Henry's only decision in a short and unremarkable career. Nonetheless, Henry and his brother combined to win 372 games.

⚾ ⚾ ⚾

Who holds the National League record for consecutive innings without allowing a base on balls?

New York Giants right-hander Christy Mathewson set a National League record in 1913 by tossing 68 consecutive innings without allowing a base on balls. San Diego Padres southpaw Randy Jones tied Mathewson's mark in 1976. Atlanta Braves right-hander Greg Maddux passed both hurlers on August 7, 2001. Maddux didn't walk a batter in his six innings of play, reaching 70 $\frac{1}{3}$ consecutive innings without allowing a free pass. He left the game for a pinch-hitter in the bottom of the sixth with his streak in tact. Five days later Maddux was closing in on Kansas City Athletics righty Bill Fischer's 1962 major league record of 84 $\frac{1}{3}$ innings. Maddux threw two more innings without walking a batter, but the Diamondbacks were threatening to score in the top of the third inning. The Braves pitching star looked in the dugout as manager Bobby Cox put up four fingers, indicating he wanted the batter intentionally walked. Maddux threw four outside pitches, ending his streak on an intentional walk. The

Braves ace later said, "If I was the manager, I would have walked him too."

Baltimore Orioles third baseman Brook Robinson is generally regarded as the best defensive third basemen in the history of the game. The "human vacuum cleaner" won 16 consecutive Gold Gloves from 1960–1975. (Bettmann/Corbis)

Chapter Three

Fielding Gems

"The secret to my pitching success?
Clean living and a fast outfield."
—Lefty Gomez

Triple Plays

How many unassisted triple plays have occurred in the modern era?

Unassisted triple plays are among the rarest of defensive gems. The first unassisted triple play of the modern era occurred on July 19, 1909. In the top of the second inning of the first game of a doubleheader, the visiting Boston Red Sox had Jake Stahl on first base and Heinie Wagner on second base with nobody out. The batter, Amby McConnell, hit a line drive caught by Cleveland Naps shortstop Neal Ball, who stepped on second base and tagged the runner coming from first. Ball had committed 81 errors the prior season, but he managed to pull off a memorable play on this day.

The last unassisted triple play occurred on May 29, 2000, when the Oakland Athletics visited Yankee Stadium. The Yankees had Jorge Posada on first base and Tino Martinez on second in the bottom of the sixth inning. Posada and Martinez were moving on the pitch as Shane Spencer smacked a line drive. Athletics second baseman Randy Velarde caught the liner, tagged Posada, and stepped on second to force out Martinez. It was the 11th and most recent unassisted triple play. American League infielders have executed seven unassisted triple plays and National League infielders have the remaining four. No pitcher, catcher, or outfielder has ever pulled off an unassisted triple play.

As rare as unassisted triple plays have been, shortstop Jimmy Cooney managed to participate in two unassisted triple plays. On May 7, 1925, Cooney was with the St. Louis Cardinals, and was on second base when Pittsburgh Pirates shortstop Glenn Wright pulled off an unassisted triple play. On May 30, 1927, Cooney was now with the Chicago Cubs, and he pulled off an unassisted triple play against the Pittsburgh Pirates. Cooney is the only player in baseball history to have been involved in two unassisted triple plays, one as a base runner and the other as a fielder.

What are the shortest and longest times between unassisted triple plays?

What was the shortest time? One Year? One Month? One week? On May 30, 1927, the Chicago Cubs visited the Pittsburgh Pirates to play a Memorial Day double-header. In the bottom of the fourth inning of the opener, the Pirates had Clyde Barnett on first base and Lloyd Waner on second with no out. Paul Waner, brother of Lloyd, hit a line drive that was caught by Cubs shortstop Jimmy Cooney. Cooney stepped on second base to force out Lloyd, and tagged Barnett for the third out. That was the sixth unassisted triple play in baseball history. Fans wouldn't have to wait too long for the seventh.

On the very next day the Cleveland Indians were on the road against the Detroit Tigers. In the top of the ninth inning, the Indians had two men on base with nobody out. Tigers first baseman Johnny Neun caught a line drive hit by Homer Summa. Neun tagged the runner who had moved off first base, and then touched a vacated second base for the third out. It was a game-ending triple play that preserved a 1–0 victory for the Tigers. Unassisted triple plays on consecutive days are unparalleled in the annals of baseball history. When would the next one happen? One year? Five years? Ten years?

Decades would pass before fans would witness another unassisted triple play. On July 30, 1968, Washington Senators shortstop Ron Hansen executed an unassisted triple play against the Cleveland Indians. The Indians had runners on first and second base, and were running with the pitch. Hansen caught a line drive hit by Joe Azcue, stepped on second for a force out, and tagged the runner coming from first. Forty-one years is the longest time between unassisted triple plays. So Neun's unassisted triple play came one day after Cooney's and 41 years before Hansen's.

⚾ ⚾ ⚾

How many unassisted triple plays have occurred in a World Series?

The 1920 World Series may have been the most important of Fall Classics. Memories of the infamous "Black Sox Scandal" were fresh in the minds and hearts of baseball fans everywhere. One week before the '20 Series was about to begin, a Grand Jury accused eight players from the Chicago White Sox team of accepting bribes to rig the 1919 World Series. Another tragic event occurred less than two months earlier when Indians shortstop Ray Chapman was hit in the head and killed by a pitch thrown by New York Yankees right-hander Carl Mays. Playing under these clouds, the Cleveland Indians faced the Brooklyn Robins in the 1920 World Series.

The Series was tied at two games apiece as the teams squared off in Game Five. The Robins had two men on base and nobody out in the top of the fifth inning. Clarence Mitchell came to bat and hit a wicked line drive to the left of second base. Indians second baseman Bill Wambsganss made a leaping catch of the liner, stepped on a vacated second base for a force out, and tagged the runner coming from first to pull off the unassisted triple play.

Years later "Wamby" said, "Funny thing, I played in the big leagues for 13 years and the only thing anyone seems to remember is that once I made an unassisted triple play in the World Series." He might have been surprised, but his unassisted triple play remains the only one in a World Series.

🅐 🅐 🅐

Which team hit into two triple plays in one game?

No team relishes the idea of hitting into a triple play. So imagine how the Boston Red Sox felt on July 17, 1990. The Red Sox had the bases loaded and nobody out in the bottom of the fourth inning when cleanup hitter Tom Brunansky grounded to Minnesota Twins third baseman Gary Gaetti. Gaetti stepped on third, threw to second baseman Al Newman, who in turn relayed to first baseman Kent Hrbek to complete the triple play.

The Red Sox futility at the plate continued. In the bottom of the eighth inning, they had runners on first and second with nobody out when Jody Reed hit a ground ball to Gaetti. The Twins third baseman again started a round-the-horn triple play. The Red Sox became the first and only team in baseball history to hit into two triple plays in one game. Despite their offensive lapses, the Red Sox won 1–0.

On the very next day the Red Sox offense sputtered once again, but Twins batters also failed to produce at the plate. The teams combined to hit into 10 double plays, setting another major league record. The Red

Sox hit into six of the double plays and the Twins the remaining four. Once again the Red Sox managed to pull off a victory. In more than a century of major league baseball, only once has a team hit into two triple plays in a game and only once have two teams combined to hit into 10 double plays in one game—and these records occurred on consecutive days.

Fielding Feats

How can a runner be credited with a stolen base and a caught stealing on the same play?

It might be difficult to imagine how this could happen but on June 19, 1991, Atlanta Braves shortstop Rafael Belliard managed to register a stolen base and caught stealing on the same play in a game against the Philadelphia Phillies. Belliard was on first base and Greg Olson was on third in the top of the sixth inning when the batter, Tom Glavine, missed a bunt attempt. Belliard got to second base on the play, but Olsen got hung up in a rundown between third and home. Eventually Olsen and Belliard ended up on third base together. So Belliard ran back toward second and Olson headed for home, but Olson got into another rundown between third and home. Once again, both Olson and Belliard headed to third base, and this time Belliard was tagged out. It may be confusing, but officially Belliard was caught stealing at third base, but he also was credited with a steal for going from first to second on the play.

$$\bigcirc \bigcirc \bigcirc$$

How can a runner be caught stealing twice in one at-bat?

Although it doesn't occur too often, consider what happened to Pittsburgh Pirates first baseman Jeff King on June 15, 1992. King led off the fifth inning with a single against Philadelphia Phillies southpaw Terry Mulholland, and a subsequent pickoff throw by Phillies catcher Darren Daulton trapped King between first and second base. Mulholland almost ran into King when he tried to get back to first, and Mulholland was called for interference. King was ruled safe because of the interference, but was officially charged with a caught stealing. Later in the inning King was thrown out as he tried to steal third base. Thus, King was caught stealing twice in one at-bat. It's possible for a runner to be caught stealing more than twice in one at-bat, but it hasn't happened yet.

$$\bigcirc \bigcirc \bigcirc$$

Who played catcher for both Babe Ruth and Ted Williams?

Babe Ruth and Ted Williams are regarded by many as the greatest hitters in the history of the game, but they are tied together in way that has nothing to do with their batting accomplishments. "The Bambino" was a superb hurler for the Boston Red Sox. In 1916 Ruth went 23–12 with an American League leading 1.75 ERA. The following season, he registered a 24–13 record with a 2.01 ERA. Ruth also pitched a few games for the Yankees near the end of his career. He had a lifetime record of 94–46, including a 5–0 mark as a Yankee. Ruth made his last pitching appearance on the final day of the 1933 season, and his battery-mate was Yankees catcher Joe Glenn.

Williams, on the other hand, pitched only one game in his lengthy career. He tossed two innings against the visiting Detroit Tigers on August 24, 1940. Williams' catcher that day was none other than Joe Glenn. So Glenn caught in Ruth's last pitching appearance and Williams's only pitching appearance.

⚾ ⚾ ⚾

What defensive strategy did Lou Boudreau use against Ted Williams?

Cleveland Indians player/manager Lou Boudreau devised a defensive shift that he hoped would slow down the legendary Ted Williams. The "Boudreau Shift" was first used on July 14, 1946, when the Indians visited Boston's Fenway Park to play a doubleheader against the Red Sox. Boudreau slammed four doubles and a homer in the opener of the twin bill, but was outdone by Williams, who led his team to an 11–10 victory with three home runs and eight RBIs. Boudreau could not have been pleased.

In the second game of the doubleheader, Boudreau instructed his players to take an unorthodox position on the diamond against Williams. The Indians manager moved his third baseman to the right of second base. Boudreau, who was the Indians shortstop, stood midway between first base and second base. His second baseman stood in short right field not too far from the right field foul line. Boudreau positioned his first baseman behind the first base bag adjacent to the right field line. His centerfielder and right fielder shifted sharply to the right. The defense was set as the Red Sox slugger came to the plate.

Williams walked on four pitches!

Which defensive player blew on a ball?

Many fielders stretch, jump, or dive to make a key defensive play, but at least one infielder attempted to blow at a ball. On May 27, 1981, Seattle Mariners third baseman Lenny Randle did some quick thinking in a game against the Kansas City Royals. In the top of the sixth inning, Royals speedster Amos Otis hit a slow ground ball along the third base line. Randle realized he didn't have a play at first base, and he attempted to blow the ball into foul territory. Royals manager Whitey Herzog protested, but Randle claimed he was simply pleading for the ball to go foul. Umpire Larry McCoy ruled that it was a fair ball despite Randle's plea, and Otis was credited with a single. Nonetheless, Randle's defensive ingenuity merits recognition.

How can a team have three or more sacrifice flies in one inning?

It can occur only if a defensive player commits an error. Consider what happened to the Chicago White Sox when they faced the Cleveland Indians in the second game of a doubleheader on July 1, 1962. A sacrifice fly brought in a run on a fly ball putout to Indians right fielder Gene Green. But Green committed errors on the next two fly balls, each resulting in a sacrifice fly. In both cases the scorekeeper ruled that the runner on third base would have scored regardless of Green's misplays. The White Sox became the first team in major league history to register three sacrifice flies in one inning.

Fielding Records and Awards

Who was the first outfielder to throw out three base runners at home plate in one game?

It's tough enough to throw out one or two base runners at home plate in a game, but how often does an outfielder do it three times in the same contest? On June 19, 1889, William "Dummy" Hoy of the Washington Senators became the first of only three outfielders to have accomplished this feat when he threw out three Indianapolis Hoosiers at the plate. Hoy was probably in position to get the assists since he typically played a shallow center field. His great speed and powerful arm also helped to make him a solid defensive outfielder.

Hoy received his nickname because he was deaf-mute. Despite his handicap, he had an impressive 14-year career. Hoy smacked more than 2,000 hits, scored a hundred or more runs nine times, and stole 594 bases. (In those days runners were credited with a steal for taking an extra base, such as going from first to third on a single.) Hoy also hit the first grand slam home run in American League history on May 1, 1901.

When Hoy was at the plate he had to read the umpire's lips in order to find out whether the pitch was called a "ball" or "strike." His average dropped sharply one season when opposing hurlers quick-pitched him. Hoy's average climbed again when he had his third base coach signal whether a pitch was either a "ball" or "strike." Soon after Hoy's experience, umpires started using hand and arm gestures in addition to verbal calls to indicate "balls" and "strikes." Legend has it that Hoy influenced the change by umpires.

⚾ ⚾ ⚾

What is the major league record for errorless games in a season by a catcher?

Catchers play the most physically demanding position in the field. An errant pickoff throw or dropped pop fly behind home plate might occur at any moment in a game, thereby making the possibility of a lengthy errorless streak minimal. Florida Marlins backstop Charles Johnson was up to the task in 1997 as he played in a total of 124 games without committing a single error. Johnson's errorless streak actually began during the 1996 season, and ended on opening day of the '98 season.

During that time he played 172 consecutive regular season errorless games, his second major league record. It's hard to imagine a catcher going a full year without committing an error, but Johnson's streak lasted more than the equivalent of an entire season.

⚾ ⚾ ⚾

What is the major league record for errorless games in a season by a first baseman?

Steve Garvey played third base for the Los Angeles Dodgers early in his career, but his erratic play at the "hot corner" caused the team to move him to first base. It turned out to be a wise decision. Garvey became an outstanding defensive first baseman, winning the National League Gold Glove from 1974 to 1977. The All-Star first baseman became a free agent at the end of the 1982 season, and signed a five-year contract with the San Diego Padres.

In 1984 Garvey may have had his most outstanding season in the field. He played a major league record of 160 games for the Padres at first base without committing a single error. Despite Garvey's superb defensive play, New York Mets first basemen Keith Hernandez took home one of his 11 consecutive Gold Gloves.

⚾ ⚾ ⚾

What is the major league record for errorless games in a season by an outfielder?

Rocky Colavito broke in with the Cleveland Indians in 1955 and rapidly became a fan favorite. Colavito had productive seasons in 1956 and 1957 and emerged as one of the best hitters in the American League over the next couple of years. In 1958 he batted .303 with 41 home runs and 113 RBIs. The following season Colavito hit a league-leading 42 homers and drove in 111 runs. On June 10, 1959, he became only the fourth player in baseball history to hit four consecutive homers in one game.

Colavito's career was taking off when, one day prior to the start of the 1960 season, general manager Frank Lane infuriated Indians fans by trading the popular outfielder to the Detroit Tigers. After five impressive seasons, including one with the Kansas City Athletics, the beloved Colavito returned to the "Tribe" in 1965. Colavito played 162 games that year without committing a single error. He also excelled at the plate during the '65 season, leading all American League hitters with 93 bases on balls and 108 RBIs. Cleveland's fans were thrilled to have Colavito back in an Indians uniform.

Which pitcher won 16 consecutive Gold Gloves?

Southpaw Jim Kaat was a superb pitcher who won nearly 300 games in his major-league best 25-year career. In addition to having success on the mound, Kaat excelled in the field. His quickness and agility helped him to stand out defensively. Kaat won the American League Gold Glove as a Minnesota Twin from 1962 to 1972. He started the 1973 season with the Twins, but was traded to the Chicago White Sox. Kaat continued his streak with the White Sox, winning three more AL Gold Gloves from 1973 to 1975. But the big lefty would soon be moving to another team.

On December 9, 1975, Bill Veeck headed a group that purchased a majority interest in the White Sox. On the following day, Veeck traded Kaat to the Philadelphia Phillies. Kaat continued to play stellar defense as a member of the Phillies, winning the National League Gold Glove in 1976 and 1977. That adds up to an impressive 16 consecutive Gold Gloves. Kaat is often regarded as the best fielding pitcher in the history of the game.

⚾ ⚾ ⚾

Which 16-time Gold Glove winner committed three errors in one inning?

It wasn't Jim Kaat. Baltimore Orioles Hall of Fame third baseman Brooks Robinson won 16 consecutive Gold Gloves from 1960 to 1975. But Robinson proved one summer day that he too was human. On

July 28, 1971, he committed three errors in the sixth inning against the Oakland Athletics. Despite a poor outing, Robinson was one of the best, if not the best, defensive third basemen in baseball history. He registered the best fielding percentage, most putouts, most assists, most double plays, and many other career records for third basemen.

Robinson became known as the "human vacuum cleaner" since he made spectacular defensive plays on an almost daily basis. Former manager Sparky Anderson said, "I'm beginning to see Brooks in my sleep. If I dropped this paper plate, he'd pick it up on one hop and throw me out at first."

Right-handed pinch-hitter Eddie Gaedel, who was three feet and seven inches tall, came into the game as a promotional stunt by St. Louis Browns' owner Bill Veeck. Gaedel walked on four consecutive pitchers in his only big-league appearance.
(Bettmann/Corbis)

Chapter Four

Extra Innings

"They throw the ball, I hit it; they
hit the ball, I catch it."
—Willie Mays

Baseball Bonanza

Which player was traded for himself?

How can a player be traded for himself? In transactions between teams, one player can be traded for another player "to be named later." In other words, when some trades are made, team A will send a player to Team B immediately, and the two teams can decide later which player from Team B will be sent to Team A. If the player-to-be-named-later turns out to be the same one who was traded for originally, then that player would be traded for himself.

That's exactly what happened to catcher Harry Chiti. The Cleveland Indians traded Chiti to the New York Mets on April 25, 1962 for a player-to-be-named-later. He played 15 games for the Mets and batted .195, and the Mets front office decided that he was expendable. The deal of April 25 was completed on June 15 when the Mets sent Chiti back to the Indians as the player-to-be-named-later. Chiti was traded for himself!

🏐 🏐 🏐

Who scored 33 runs without ever coming to bat?

Oakland Athletics manager Charles Finley signed world-class sprinter Herb Washington to a contract in 1974 for the sole purpose of running the bases. Washington was a track star who held the world indoor record for the 60-yard dash, but he hadn't played baseball since his high school days. The lack of experience may have hurt the speedster's chance at success on the base path.

In Washington's 105 game career with the Athletics, he scored 33 runs, stole 31 bases, and was caught stealing 17 times. His 65 percent rate of success on the base paths was less than stellar, and he couldn't contribute to the team in any other way since he never came to bat and never played the field. Washington was released by the Athletics in 1975.

🏐 🏐 🏐

How did the "Black Sox" originally get their nickname?

The infamous Black Sox Scandal occurred in the 1919 World Series between the Cincinnati Reds and the heavily favored Chicago White Sox. The White Sox showcased stars such as "Shoeless" Joe Jackson, Eddie Collins, Buck Weaver, Lefty Williams and Eddie Cicotte. Much to almost everyone's surprise, the Reds defeated the White Sox 5–3 in a best-of-nine series. Rumors swirled that the Series had been fixed, and one year later eight White Sox players were indicted by a Cook County Grand Jury. Although acquitted of the charges, newly empowered Baseball Commissioner Judge Kenesaw Mountain Landis ruled that their involvement in throwing the Series merited lifetime banishment from baseball. When reference is made to the Black Sox, it is about members of the 1919 White Sox.

But that is not how they *originally* got the name "Black Sox." White Sox owner Charles Comiskey was among the stingiest of team owners. Comiskey paid his players disproportionately low salaries, causing resentment among many on the team. The miserly owner stooped to a new low when he refused to pay laundry costs for cleaning team uniforms. When players stopped washing their uniforms they were nicknamed the "Black Sox"—well before the scandal came to public attention.

⚾ ⚾ ⚾

Who wore the number "1/8"?

On August 19, 1951, the last-place St. Louis Browns were at home for a doubleheader against the Detroit Tigers. Innovative owner Bill Veeck, who had purchased the Browns one month earlier, was about to make one of his most memorable moves. Many of the more than 18,000 fans attended the doubleheader to celebrate the birthday of the Falstaff Brewing Company. Most received a bottle of Falstaff beer and a piece of birthday cake as they entered the stadium. The fans were in a festive mood and the best was yet to come.

In the bottom of the first inning of the nightcap, Eddie Gaedel was announced as the pinch-hitter for leadoff batter Frank Saucier. Gaedel, who was a mere three feet and seven inches tall, wore the number "1/8" on his uniform. Tigers manager Red Rolfe protested Gaedel's presence, but umpire Ed Hurley had earlier approved Gaedel's entry into the game.

A bemused Tigers left-hander Bob Cain walked Gaedel on four straight pitches. Gaedel was immediately replaced by a pinch-runner and slowly walked backed toward the dugout to a cheering crowd. That was Gaedel's only plate appearance in the only game of his major league career. Two days later the AL banned Gaedel from baseball, but he would not soon be forgotten.

⚾ ⚾ ⚾

Who was "Bonehead" Merkle?

The New York Giants and Chicago Cubs were battling for the National League pennant late into the 1908 season. The two teams faced off in a critical contest on September 23 at the Giants' Polo Grounds. Unfortunately for the home team, their starting first baseman Fred Tenney was injured and unable to play.

(It turned out to be the only game that Tenney missed all season.) Giants manager John McGraw replaced Tenney with 19-year-old Fred Merkle, who was making his first major league start. The clubs were tied 1–1 with two out in the bottom of the ninth inning, but the Giants were threatening with Merkle on first base and Harry McCormick on third. Al Bridwell followed with a clutch single, and as McCormack scored the apparent winning run, Merkle trotted off the field. Giants fans joyously ran on to the field.

But Cubs second baseman Johnny Evers noticed that Merkle never touched second base, thereby keeping alive the possibility of a force out. In the confusion, Evers retrieved the ball that was hit by Bridwell (or what was alleged to be the ball) and stepped on second for an apparent force out to end the inning without the winning run scoring. What's the ruling? Later that evening, umpire Hank O'Day decided the run didn't count and the game was declared a tie. National League president Harry Pulliam ruled that the contest would have to be replayed if necessary.

It was necessary. The Giants and Cubs ended the season deadlocked. A replay of the "Merkle" game took place on October 8 at the Giants' Polo Grounds. Unfortunately for the home team, the Cubs won the game and clinched the NL pennant. Merkle's error in judgment apparently cost the Giants a pennant, and earned him the nickname "Bonehead." Although Merkle shouldered the responsibility for what occurred, why didn't McGraw or one of his players alert the young first baseman to touch second base? Merkle went on to have an accomplished major league career, but he never lived down that fateful day in September.

In fairness to Merkle, his failure to touch second base in that situation was not at all uncommon in the early days of baseball. On September 4 of that season, a play occurred that reflects on the attitude of other ballplayers at the time. The visiting Cubs visited the Pittsburgh Pirates, who were also in the middle of the pennant race. The teams were scoreless in the bottom of the 10th inning when the Pirates loaded the bases with two out. Warren Gill was on first base and Fred Clarke was on third when Al Bridwell singled to score Clarke with what seemed to be the winning run. Like Merkle, Gill stopped before touching second base and headed for the dugout. Evers retrieved the ball, stepped on second, and claimed the force out ended the inning without the run scoring.

Umpire O'Day, the same umpire from Merkle's infamous game, already left the field. When told what happened, O'Day allowed the winning run to score in what seemed to be a situation identical to the one Merkle in which found himself nearly one month later.

⚾ ⚾ ⚾

What was special about the way John Kruk retired from the game?

First baseman and outfielder John Kruk was a superb hitter throughout his 10 year career. The colorful Kruk played in exactly 1,200 games and had a lifetime batting average of exactly .300 with exactly 100 home runs. He also was a three-time All-Star, but may have saved his most memorable moment in baseball for last. Kruk was the designated hitter for the Chicago White Sox on July 30, 1995, when he hit a single in the top of the first inning off Baltimore Orioles right-hander Scott Erickson. That would be Kruk's last appearance in a major league game.

Kruk intended to retire from baseball in a way that virtually no one in the ballpark could have anticipated. Although White Sox manager Terry Bevington had advance knowledge of Kruk's plan, the remainder of the team was unaware of what was about to happen. Kruk was immediately replaced by a pinch-runner. He went into the dugout, said goodbye to his teammates, and left Baltimore's Camden Yards with his awaiting family. The charismatic ballplayer retired on his own terms.

⚾ ⚾ ⚾

Who umpired and singled in the same game?

Only one umpire took the field in the early days of baseball. If the umpire was unable to call a game, then each team would pick a player to do the job. On August 20, 1901, umpire Bob Emsley called the first end of a doubleheader between the Philadelphia Phillies and Brooklyn Superbas, but he became ill before the second contest and was unable to continue. As a result, Phillies pitcher Al Orth and Superbas catcher Jim McGuire took over his duties. In the ninth inning, the Phillies were down a couple of runs, and Orth was needed as a pinch-hitter. He stroked a single and later scored. Despite Orth's yeoman work, the squad from Brooklyn edged out a victory.

Who played for three different managers in three consecutive games?

Catcher Matt Nokes started the 1990 season with the Detroit Tigers, but manager Sparky Anderson was concerned about his erratic play behind the plate. Nokes played his last game with the Tigers on June 3, when he was traded to the New York Yankees. He played his first game for the Bronx Bombers on June 3, and went 1–3 as the designated hitter for manager Bucky Dent. Dent, who managed the Yankees for only 89 games, was fired the following day. He was replaced by Stump Merrill, who had managed the Columbus farm team. Nokes was behind the plate for Merrill's managerial debut, thereby playing for his third manager in three games.

Who was the youngest major league ball player?

Cincinnati Reds left-hander Joe Nuxhall pitched two-thirds of an inning in an 18–0 loss to the St. Louis Cardinals on June 10, 1944. He gave up five runs on two hits and five walks in his brief appearance. Nuxhall was 15 years, 10 months, and 11 days old, the youngest major leaguer in baseball history. He would not have been allowed to play that day unless the Reds got permission from Nuxhall's high school principal. The young pitcher's next game was eight years later in 1952. Nuxhall compiled a 135–117 record in his 16-year career.

⚾ ⚾ ⚾

Who was the oldest major league ballplayer?

Cleveland Indians owner Bill Veeck was thought to have pulled off a publicity stunt when he signed 42-year-old right-hander Satchel Paige to a contract in 1948. Paige had been a charismatic star in the Negro Leagues for decades, and is regarded by many who observed him as the greatest pitcher of all time. He pitched in exhibition games against major league All-Stars such as Babe Ruth and Rogers Hornsby. After one of those games, New York Yankee legend Joe DiMaggio said Paige was "The best I've ever faced, and the fastest."

Paige made his major league debut in a relief appearance on July 9, 1948. Although there is some uncertainty about his actual date of birth, most baseball records state that Paige was born on July 7, 1906. If that birth date is accurate, then the 42-year-old Paige became the oldest rookie in the history of the game.

Seventeen years later, on September 25, 1965, Paige made a brief appearance for the Kansas City Athletics. He pitched three scoreless innings against the Boston

Red Sox at the tender age of 59, becoming the oldest player to make a major league appearance. In 1971 the Special Committee on the Negro Leagues elected Paige to the Hall of Fame.

⚾ ⚾ ⚾

What were the most brothers from one family to play major league baseball?

A number of families, including the DiMaggio clan, had three brothers play big league ball, but the Delahanty family surpassed that number. Ed Delahanty was the most accomplished ballplayer of the group. "Big Ed" played 16 seasons from 1887 to 1903, and batted over .400 on three occasions for the Philadelphia Phillies. In 1945 he was elected by the Veterans Committee to the Hall of Fame. Ed once said of himself and his brothers that "We were given bats instead of rattles." In that case, his parents had to purchase seven bats.

Brother Jim made his major league debut in 1901 and played for eight teams in his 11-year career. Joe was an outfielder and second baseman for the St. Louis Cardinals from 1907 to 1909. Frank was an outfielder who saw limited action with the New York Yankees and Cleveland Indians from 1905 to 1908. Lastly, Tom played a total of 14 games in 1884 and 1886 to 1887. Two other brothers never played major league baseball. No other family has had as many as five brothers in the big leagues.

Who fell asleep in center field?

On June 8, 1920, the Cincinnati Reds visited the Polo Grounds to play the New York Giants. A lengthy dispute ensued at one point in the game. As a result, Reds center fielder Edd Roush decided to lie down in the outfield. As the argument raged on, Roush managed to fall asleep. Once the dispute was settled, Reds third baseman Heinie Groh went to awaken his teammate. But the umpire ejected Roush for delaying the game.

Pitching Oddities

Which National League pitcher never played in a major league game?

The National League is, of course, one of the two major leagues. So how could this happen? Rather, how did it happen? The Milwaukee Braves visited the Houston Astros on September 15, 1971, and Larry Yount, older brother of Hall of Famer Robin, was announced as the new pitcher for the Astros in the top of the ninth inning. Unfortunately, Larry injured himself during warm-ups, and another pitcher came in to face the Braves. That turned out to be the only "appearance" in Larry's abbreviated major league career. Statistically, he "played" in that game since he was announced as the new pitcher. His official statistics state that he played one game for the Astros. Thus, Larry never played *in* a major league game, but he was a National League player for one game according to the records of Major League Baseball.

⚾ ⚾ ⚾

Which pitcher won a game without throwing a pitch?

A hurler can be credited with a win only if he gets an out, but a pitch need not be thrown to register an out. The Baltimore Orioles visited the Detroit Tigers on May 1, 2003, and the Orioles trailed 2–1 with two out in the bottom of the seventh inning. Utility infielder Omar Infante was on first base when Orioles reliever B. J. Ryan entered the game. Before throwing his first pitch Ryan attempted to pick off Infante, who took off for second base. Orioles first baseman Jeff Conine caught Ryan's throw, and immediately threw to the shortstop for a putout at second to end the inning. Infante was charged with a caught stealing.

The Orioles rallied to score three runs in the top of the eighth inning, taking a 4–2 lead. Ryan became the pitcher of record on the winning side, and would register a victory if the Orioles did not relinquish the lead. Left-hander Buddy Groom relieved Ryan to start the bottom of the eighth inning and retired the side in order. Right-hander Jorge Julio relieved Groom in the bottom of the ninth and retired the side without ever surrendering the lead. Ryan was credited with his third victory of the season despite not having thrown a single pitch.

Which pitcher was struck by lightning?

In 1910 right-hander Ray Caldwell broke into the major leagues with the New York Highlanders (soon to become the Yankees), and spent the first nine years of his career with the team. In 1919 Caldwell was traded to the Boston Red Sox and then the Cleveland Indians. On August 24, 1919, Caldwell made his debut with the Indians a memorable one. During the contest, he was struck by a bolt of lightning that sent him reeling. Despite the thunderous blow, Caldwell quickly recovered and continued pitching. To the surprise of all, he completed the game, defeating the Philadelphia Athletics.

Caldwell apparently recuperated from any injury he might have suffered, as he tossed a no-hitter against the Yankees two weeks later.

⚾ ⚾ ⚾

Which pitcher talked to the ball?

Right-hander Mark Fidrych made his major league debut for the Detroit Tigers on April 20, 1976. In his first big league start on May 15, Fidrych took a perfect game into the fifth inning and settled for a two-hitter as the Tigers beat the Cleveland Indians 2–1. "The Bird" talked to the ball throughout the game and rapidly became a fan favorite in Detroit. His popularity would soon spread throughout the country.

Six weeks later, a national television audience witnessed Fidrych talking to the ball, stomping around the infield, smoothing out the mound, shaking hands with his teammates after great defensive plays—and pitching great baseball. Fidrych gave up a solo home run to Yankees catcher Ellie Hendricks and didn't walk a single batter as he defeated the visiting New York Yankees 5–1 for his seventh consecutive victory. Fans would not leave the stadium after the game unless Fidrych took a curtain call. The Bird returned to the field to thunderous applause, and baseball had a new hero.

Fidrych went 19–9 for the season, leading the American League with 24 complete games and a 2.34 ERA. He was named American League Rookie of the Year and finished second to Baltimore Orioles ace Jim Palmer in the voting for the Cy Young Award. The Bird seemed destined for greatness, but an injury during spring training prior to the '77 season caused irreparable damage to his arm. Fidrych would win only 10 more games in his career and retired at the end of the 1980 season.

What are the fewest number of batters a pitcher must face to be credited with a complete game?

A starting pitcher must face a minimum of 24 or 27 batters in a complete nine-inning game, but many contests are cut short by rain or other factors. An official game must go at least four-and-a-half innings with the home team ahead, or five innings with the visiting team leading. If the home team has the lead after four and a half innings, then they need not bat in the bottom of the fifth inning. So a winning pitcher must face a minimum of 15 batters in a five-inning complete game victory. But the answer is "13." Why?

Consider a game pitched by Kansas City Royals right-hander Dick Drago against the Baltimore Orioles on July 30, 1971. Drago gave up a solo homer to Frank Robinson in the bottom of the first inning, but he retired the remaining 12 Orioles batters over the first four innings. Rain halted the contest after four and a half innings as Orioles right-hander Jim Palmer recorded a 1–0 victory. Drago was the losing pitcher, but he was credited with a complete game after having faced a mere 13 batters.

Only the losing pitcher of a visiting team can accomplish this feat, and Drago is the only hurler in baseball history to have tossed a 13-batter complete game.

How can a pitcher have more shutouts than complete games?

It's generally assumed that any shutout must be a complete game, but that's not the case. The rulebook states that "No pitcher shall be credited with pitching a shutout unless he pitches the complete game, or unless he enters the game with none out before the opposing team has scored in the first inning, puts out the side without a run scoring and pitches all the rest of the game" (see rule 10.19[f]). Thus, a pitcher can toss a shutout without throwing a complete game. If the pitcher does not register a complete during the season, then he'll have more shutouts than complete games.

This actually happened to New York Yankees right-hander Neil Allen. On May 31, 1988, Yankees southpaw Al Leiter faced the Oakland Athletics. Unfortunately, Leiter was injured on his very first pitch when the Athletics' leadoff batter, Carney Lansford, smacked a single that hit the Yankees pitcher. Allen relieved for the injured starter, retired the next three batters without a run scoring, and tossed eight more innings of shutout ball. Allen was credited with a shutout, but not a complete game. He pitched in 41 games during the '88 season, including two starts, no complete games, and one shutout.

Allen is the only pitcher in baseball history to have more shutouts than complete games in a season.

How can a pitcher have more shutouts than victories?

Many games were called due to rain or darkness in the early days of baseball. Some of those contests result-ed in ties, and a couple of those ties were shutouts. Thus, a pitcher could toss a shutout without gaining a victory. If that hurler failed to win any games during the season, then he would have more shutouts than victories. At least four pitchers have had such a season. The first time was in 1911 when St. Louis Cardinals right-hander Grover Lowdermilk finished the year with a record of 0–1, including a 0–0 shutout-tie. The last hurler to have more shutouts than victories in a season was Kansas City Athletics left-hander Rip Coleman, who completed the 1957 season with a record of 0–7, including one complete game shutout-tie.

⚾ ⚾ ⚾

Which pitcher led the major leagues in victories despite not playing for either a National League or American League team?

Baseball historians are well aware there was a time when three major leagues competed for the attention of baseball fans. In 1914 the Federal League became the third major league. The FL fielded eight teams, each with its own new ballpark. In order to put big league talent on their squads, FL owners raided players from the National League and American League. Some of the notable talents who jumped to the new league were "Chief" Bender, Joe Tinker, Eddie Plank, Edd Roush and Mordecai "Three-Finger" Brown—each of whom has been enshrined in the Hall of Fame.

During the 1914 season, Philadelphia Phillies right-hander Grover Cleveland Alexander led all NL hurlers with 27 victories. Washington Senators right-hander Walter Johnson took the AL title, notching 28 wins.

But another righty, Claude Hendrix, won 29 games for the Chicago Whalers of the FL to lead all major league hurlers.

Also that year, Benny Kauff played for the Indianapolis Hoosiers of the FL and led the majors with a .370 average. The FL was disbanded at the end of the 1915 season.

⚾ ⚾ ⚾

Has it ever been legal to throw a spitball?

The spitball became popular at the turn of the twentieth century and nothing in the rulebook barred its use. Two of the leading spitball pitchers were Jack Chesbro and Ed Walsh, who happen to be the only 40-game winners in baseball history. Right-hander Walsh won 40 games for the Chicago White Sox in 1908. Chesbro set the major league mark with 41 wins for the New York Highlanders (later the Yankees) in 1904. Their use of the spitball was perfectly legal.

The spitball was eventually banned in 1920, but the following year a grandfather clause was added that allowed a lifetime exemption for 17 official spitball pitchers. The last legal spitballer, future Hall of Famer Burleigh Grimes, retired from the game in 1934, but the spitball did not disappear from the game upon his retirement. It's a pitch that has continued to be thrown decades after its banishment, and many later spitball pitchers are currently enshrined in Cooperstown. Hall of Fame right-hander Gaylord Perry admitted throwing the spitter throughout his 22-year career. St. Louis Cardinals star Stan "The Man" Musial had an answer for the spitball saying that "When a pitcher's throwing a spitball, don't worry and don't complain, just hit the dry side."

Team Records

Which team had the best record in baseball but failed to make the playoffs?

How could a team with the best record miss the playoffs? In the early part of the 1981 season an unresolved dispute between players and owners regarding free-agent compensation threatened a disruption of play. On June 12, players union leader Marvin Miller proclaimed, "The strike is on," and major league baseball came to a screeching halt. After two long months the dispute was settled, and teams resumed play on August 10. As a result of the nearly two-month hiatus, owners decided to split the 1981 season into two halves with the first place teams from each half in each division playing each other.

The Cincinnati Reds were 35–21 and finished one half game behind the Los Angeles Dodgers in the first half of the National League season. The Reds went 31–21 and finished one and a half games behind the Houston Astros in the second half. Despite compiling an NL best record of 66–42, they did not "win" either half of the season, and thus did not qualify for post-season play. Moreover, they had the best overall record of any major league team in 1981, but it was little consolation to the Reds and their fans.

⚾ ⚾ ⚾

What was the smallest margin of victory for a pennant-winning team?

The 1908 American League pennant race went down to the wire as the Detroit Tigers, Cleveland Indians, and Chicago White Sox battled until the very end of the season. Tigers right-hander "Wild Bill" Donovan shut out the Chisox on the final day of play, allowing Detroit to clinch the American League pennant. The Tigers completed the season with a 90–63 record, and edged out the Indians who finished at 90–64. Detroit won the American League pennant by a mere half game. (The Tigers were not required to make up an earlier rainout.) Third place went to the White Sox who were one and a half back at 88–64. The half-game margin of victory is an unbeatable mark.

Current rules would not allow a team to win a pennant by a half game. If a first-place team had a half-game lead over the second-place on the last day of the season, at least one of the clubs would have to make up a cancelled game or complete a suspended game.

What was the shortest nine-inning game in baseball history?

A couple of right-handers, Jesse Barnes of the New York Giants and Lee Meadows of the Philadelphia Phillies, faced off in the first game of a doubleheader on the final day of the 1919 season. Barnes was the ace of manager John McGraw's pitching staff and entered the game with 24 victories. Meadows became a 20-game winner later in his career and also happened to be the first player in the modern era to wear glasses. Each pitcher wasted little time on this day as inning after inning rapidly passed. The Giants ended up defeating the Phillies 6–1 in a contest that lasted only 51 minutes. It turned out to be the shortest nine-inning game in baseball history.

What were the most innings played in a major league game?

A number of extra-inning contests have lasted more than 20 innings, but a genuine "marathon" took place on May 1, 1920, between the Brooklyn Dodgers and the Boston Braves. A couple of right-handers, Leon Cadore of the Dodgers and Joe Oeschger of the Braves, faced off in a game that would not soon be forgotten. The Dodgers scored a run in the fourth inning and the Braves tied it up in the fifth. Those were the last runs of the game. The score remained 1–1 through 26 innings before being called for darkness. It turned out to be the most innings played in a major league game.

Incredibly, both Oeschger and Cadore tossed complete games. Oeschger gave up nine hits, walked four, and struck out seven, whereas Cadore gave up 15 hits, walked five, and struck out six. Oeschger set a major league record as he pitched 21 consecutive shutout innings. Cadore was one scoreless frame away from matching his mound opponent. Despite their masterful performances, neither pitcher was credited with either a shutout or victory.

Which team holds the major league record for consecutive wins?

Some record books credit the 1916 New York Giants with winning 26 consecutive games, but that's not exactly what happened. The Giants played 27 games from September 7 through September 30, and they won 26 of them. On September 18, the Giants and Pittsburgh Pirates played to a 1–1 tie in the nightcap of a doubleheader. Statistics of a tie game count as part of the official record. Thus, the Giants failed to put together a 26-game winning streak. Instead, they had a 27-game unbeaten streak. The Giants did have an advantage throughout the streak. Each and every one of those games happened to have been played on their home field in the Polo Grounds.

If the 1916 Giants don't own the modern day mark for consecutive victories, then which team does hold the record? Although the Chicago White Stockings won 21 consecutive games in 1880, the Chicago Cubs hold the modern day record. On September 4, 1935, the Cubs were in third place, two and a half games behind the league-leading St. Louis Cardinals. The Cubs won that game as well as the ensuing 20 contests. Their last victory in the streak occurred on September 27, when they clinched the National League pennant. The Cubs' 21 consecutive wins without a tie established a modern day mark that stands today.

Which team holds the major league record for consecutive losses?

The 1961 Philadelphia Phillies had a very different season than the '35 Cubs. The Phillies had two seven-game losing streaks as well as an eight- and 10-game losing streak—and it was only mid-July. The worst was yet to come. The Phillies lost 23 consecutive games from July 29 to August 20, setting one of the more unenviable records in baseball history. They won the second game of a doubleheader against the Milwaukee Braves on August 20, and began a season-best four-game winning streak. It didn't help much as they finished the season in last place with 107 losses.

Which team set the major league record for most runs in a game?

On June 8, 1950, the Boston Red Sox were at home in Fenway Park to play the St. Louis Browns. The Red Sox had their batting faces on that day as Bobby Doerr slammed three homers, and Walt Dropo and Ted Williams each connected on a pair of four-baggers. Al Zarilla contributed four doubles and a single. Pitcher Chuck Stobbs walked four times in four innings. Numerous major league records were set in the contest, including leadoff hitter Clyde Vollmer coming to the plate eight times in eight innings. The Red Sox also set major league marks with 58 total bases and 29 runs in the game as they routed the Browns 29–4.

One day earlier, the Red Sox had whipped the last-place Browns 20–4. Their 49 runs in two consecutive games are a major league mark that may never be approached.

⚾ ⚾ ⚾

Which team scored the most runs in an inning?

The Boston Red Sox hold the record for most runs scored in an inning as well as most runs scored in a game. On June 18, 1953, the Detroit Tigers visited Fenway Park and faced an onslaught in the seventh inning as 23 Red Sox batters came to the plate. They collected 14 hits and six walks en route to a 17-run inning and a 23–3 victory over the Tigers. They scored the 17 runs despite the absence of legendary slugger Ted Williams who missed most of the '53 season serving as a pilot in the Korean War. His replacement, rookie Gene Stephens, set an American League record and tied a major league mark as he stroked three hits in the big inning.

What are the most combined runs scored in a game?

The Deadball Era had been over for a few years and the wind must have been blowing out at Wrigley Field on August 25, 1922, but few could have predicted the impending offensive explosion. The Chicago Cubs had two big innings early in the game, scoring 10 runs in the second inning and 14 runs in the fourth, taking a seemingly insurmountable 25–6 lead over the Philadelphia Phillies. The Cubs still had a 17-run lead after seven innings, but the Phillies battled back, scoring eight runs in the top of the eighth. Nonetheless, the Cubs maintained a commanding lead.

The Phillies' comeback continued in the ninth inning as they scored six more runs. Now trailing by only three runs, the Phillies had the bases loaded with two out and hot-hitting Bevo LeBourveau at the plate. But LeBourveau struck out with the potential winning run at home plate to end the slugfest. The Cubs won 26–23 in a game that somehow lasted a little more than three hours.

The teams combined for 49 runs on 51 hits and 23 bases on balls. The Cubs set a record for one team by scoring 26 runs in the game. Although the Cubs no longer hold that mark, the combined total of 49 runs remains a major league record.

What are the fewest combined runs scored in a doubleheader?

One! On September 5, 1913, the visiting Philadelphia Phillies defeated the Boston Braves 1–0 in the opener of a twin bill. In the second game, Phillies right-hander Grover Cleveland Alexander tossed 10 scoreless innings, but his teammates were unable to generate any offense. The game was called due to darkness and ended in a 0–0 tie. The teams combined to score a total of one run in the doubleheader. That record is virtually unbeatable.

Which team holds the major league record for fewest hits allowed in a doubleheader?

On April 12, 1992, the Boston Red Sox visited Cleveland to play a doubleheader against the Indians. Red Sox southpaw Matt Young was masterful in the opener. Despite walking seven batters and giving up two runs, Young did not allow a base hit. Unfortunately, the

Red Sox scored only one run, and Young lost the contest 2–1. To make matters worse for Young, Major League Baseball established new rules in 1991 that prevented him from being credited with an "official" no-hitter.

In the second game of the twin bill, right-hander Roger Clemens tossed a two-hitter en route to a 3–0 shutout of the Indians. Young and Clemens combined to give up a major league low of two hits in the doubleheader.

Which team played in the most consecutive doubleheaders?

Although doubleheaders are somewhat uncommon today, they were routinely scheduled throughout much of baseball history. Some teams played a string of twin bills during the season, but no team can match the performance of the 1928 Boston Braves. The Braves began a series of doubleheaders on September 4th by losing both ends to the Brooklyn Dodgers. They swept the Dodgers the following day, and then split a doubleheader against the Philadelphia Phillies. The worst was yet to come as the Braves were swept in their next five doubleheaders, including four consecutive sweeps by the New York Giants. The streak ended on September 15 with a split against the Chicago Cubs. The Braves played in a major league record nine consecutive doubleheaders.

New York Yankee right-hander Don Larsen is shown throwing the final pitch of his perfect game in Game Five of the 1956 World Series. Brooklyn Dodgers pinch hitter Dale Mitchell struck out on a called third strike. Notice Yankees shortstop Billy Martin in the background. (Bettmann/Corbis)

Chapter Five

The Fall Classic

*"It took the Anaheim Angels 42
years to win the World Series; or as
the Boston Red Sox call it, 'begin-
ners luck.'"*
—David Letterman

Who were the only teams to win a pennant without making it to the World Series?

In the early 1900s, the National League and newly created American League were engaged in a feud that caused deep hostilities. One source of conflict was the fact that AL president Ban Johnson ignored the NL's reserve clause and engaged in bidding wars for players. The bickering continued until a 1903 compromise brought about a merger between the two leagues. That agreement led to the inaugural World Series of 1903 in which the Boston Pilgrims upset the heavily favored Pittsburgh Pirates.

In 1904 the New York Giants took home the NL pennant while the Pilgrims repeated as AL champions.

The two teams were ready to take the field in what would have been the second World Series, but Giants manager John McGraw and owner John T. Brush refused to play any team from the AL. McGraw complained, "American League management has been crooked more than once." Brush adamantly opposed placing an AL team in New York, and was upset with Johnson for creating the rival New York Highlanders. McGraw and Brush resisted public pressure to play against what they called a "minor league" franchise.

There was no World Series in 1904.

Which World Series pitching record was held by Babe Ruth?

The "Sultan of Swat's" accomplishments at the plate are legendary, but Ruth also was an outstanding pitcher. Ruth won 23 games in 1916 for the Boston Red Sox, leading all American League pitchers with nine shutouts and a 1.75 ERA. In 1917 Ruth won 24 games for the Red Sox and led the league with 35 complete games. He had a career mark of 94–46 with an impressive 2.28 ERA. There is little doubt that Ruth would have achieved Hall of Fame stature as a hurler if he had remained a pitcher throughout his career.

The Red Sox though took notice of Ruth's immense ability at the plate. They wanted him to be in the lineup on a regular basis, and in 1918 Ruth began to play the outfield and an occasional first base. He tied for the American League lead in homers that season with 11. The following year Ruth slammed an astounding 29 homers. Three players tied for second best with 10 home runs, including Frank "Home Run" Baker and batting great George Sisler. Prior to the 1920 season, Ruth was traded to the New York Yankees and his pitching career was effectively over. The rest is baseball history.

Ruth's success on the mound extended to the World Series. Game Two of the 1916 World Series was one of the best pitched games in the history of the Fall Classic. Ruth defeated Brooklyn Robins left-hander Sherry Smith 2–1 in a masterfully pitched 14-inning contest. The "Babe" gave up a first-inning homer and proceeded to toss 13 shutout innings. The Red Sox won the '16 World Series in five games.

Ruth's next World Series appearance came in 1918, and in Game One he tossed a 1–0 shutout against the Chicago Cubs, extending his consecutive shutout inning streak to 22 innings. In Game Four, the "Babe" tossed seven and two thirds of shutout ball before giving up a couple of eighth inning runs. Ruth established a major league mark in World Series play with 29 $\frac{2}{3}$ consecutive shutout innings—and it lasted more than four decades. The Red Sox went on to win their fifth World Series. The team won their next World Series Championship 84 years later when they swept the Cardinals in the 2004 Fall Classic.

Which player won the most World Series championships?

It had to be a Yankee. "Yogi" Berra played in and won more World Series titles than any other player in the history of the game. The left-handed hitting catcher played in 14 World Series for the Yankees from 1947–1963, and the "Bronx Bombers" were champions in ten of those Series. Berra also managed the '64 Yankees and '74 Mets to the World Series, but those contests ended in defeat. In addition to his ten rings, Berra holds the record for hits, doubles, at-bats, and games played in the Fall Classic. For good measure, in 1947 he hit the first pinch-hit homer in World Series competition. Perhaps his most cherished moment came in the '56 World Series when he caught Don Larsen's perfect game.

Berra won the AL MVP in 1951, 1954 and 1955, and was elected to Baseball's Hall of Fame in 1972.

How many times did Ty Cobb play on a World Series Championship team?

Ty Cobb began his career with the Detroit Tigers in 1905 and dominated offensively over the next two decades. After 22 years with the Tigers, the "Georgia Peach" played his final two seasons with the Philadelphia Athletics. Cobb won 12 American League batting titles, including nine in a row from 1907 to 1915. At the time of his retirement, he held dozens of major league records. Most notably, Cobb was baseball's all-time leader in batting average, hits, stolen bases, runs scored, and games played. In 1936 Cobb became one of the five original inductees into the Baseball Hall of Fame.

Cobb's three appearances in a World Series were with the Tigers from 1907 to 1909. "Peach" had the misfortune of playing against the highly regarded Chicago Cubs, who easily defeated the Tigers to win the 1907 and 1908 World Series. The Tigers put up more of a battle in the 1909 World Series but lost in seven games to the Pittsburgh Pirates. That was the 22-year-old Cobb's last appearance in the Fall Classic. Baseball's greatest hitter for average never played on a World Series Championship team.

⚾ ⚾ ⚾

Which team made the greatest comeback in a World Series game?

The Chicago Cubs were down two games to one against the Philadelphia Athletics in the 1929 World Series, but they were on the verge of tying it up in Game Four. The Cubs had a commanding 8–0 lead as the Athletics came to bat in the bottom of the seventh inning. Athletics slugger Al Simmons began the inning with a home run. That was just the beginning—the next four Athletics batters singled. Cubs lefty Art Nehf relieved starter Charlie Root, but Nehf promptly surrendered three more runs.

Right-hander Sheriff Blake replaced Nehf, but failed to stop the onslaught as the powerful Jimmy Foxx drove in the tying run. Righty Pat Malone relieved Blake, but the Athletics scored two more runs. The Athletics ended up scoring 10 runs in the inning and defeated the Cubs 10–8. It was the greatest comeback in the history of the World Series. The Athletics also won Game Five, clinching the 1929 World Series Championship.

In which World Series did brothers win all four of their team's victories?

Dizzy and Paul Dean may be the most famous pitching brothers in baseball history. They played together for the "Gashouse Gang" St. Louis Cardinals from 1934 to 1937, and may have shared in their most memorable achievement during the 1934 World Series. Dizzy defeated the Detroit Tigers in the opener of the '34 Series as Cardinals outfielder Joe "Ducky" Medwick backed up Dean's performance with a 4–4 day.

The Tigers tied the Series with a come-from-behind victory in Game Two. Brother Paul was victorious in the third game of the Series but the Tigers bounced back to win Game Four. Although Dizzy lost the following game, Paul defeated Lynwood "Schoolboy Rowe" in Game Six to even the Series again at 3–3. Dizzy tossed an 11–0 shutout in Game Seven, clinching the 1934

World Series Championship. Paul and Dizzy combined to win all four of their team's victories in the '34 Series.

⚾ ⚾ ⚾

In which World Series did a pitcher register two wins and two saves?

In 1959 right-handed reliever Larry Sherry was called up from the minors by the Los Angeles Dodgers in the heat of a pennant race. Sherry went 7–2 down the stretch, including a playoff victory against the Milwaukee Braves, to help the Dodgers secure the National League pennant. But he wasn't done yet. Sherry was about to become the dominant force in the '59 World Series against the Chicago White Sox—despite pitching a total of only 12 ⅔ innings. After the Dodgers were pounded by the White Sox in Game One, Sherry came in to save the win in Games Two and Three. He also registered a victory in Game Four and Game Six as the Los Angeles Dodgers took home their first World Series Championship.

Sherry's performance was all the more impressive given that it was his rookie season.

⚾ ⚾ ⚾

Which team scored the most runs in a World Series?

The Pittsburgh Pirates defeated the New York Yankees 6–4 in the opener of the 1960 World Series with the help of second baseman Bill Mazeroski's two-run homer. The Bronx Bombers responded with wins in Games Two and Three by scores of 16–3 and 10–0, taking a one-game Series lead. But the Pirates bounced back to win Games Four and Five. The Yankees staved off elimination as Whitey Ford tossed his second shutout of the Series, defeating the Pirates 12–0 in Game Six.

The Pirates took an early four-run lead in Game Seven, but the Yankees rallied to go ahead 7–4 as the Bucs came to bat in the bottom of the eighth inning. The Pirates responded with a five-run outburst, taking a 9–7 lead through eight innings. But the Yankees fought back and tied the game with two runs in the top of the ninth. In the bottom of the ninth inning, the score was tied 9–9 when Mazeroski hit a leadoff home run off right-hander Bill Terry. The Pirates were World Series champions. Despite an unhappy ending, the Yankees scored a World Series best 55 runs, more than doubling the 27 runs scored by the Pirates.

Although the Pirates won the '60 Series, Yankees second baseman Bobby Richardson became the first and only player from a losing team to win a World Series MVP. It was all the more surprising since Richardson was one of the weakest hitters in a lineup filled with sluggers. Although Richardson had only one home run during the '60 season, he dominated offensively in the '60 World Series. Richardson finished with 11 hits, a .367 batting average, and a World Series record of 12 RBIs.

Which team scored the fewest runs in a World Series?

New York Giants fans were upset with management after the team was forced to boycott what would have been the 1904 World Series. In an attempt to win back fan support, owner John T. Brush and manager John McGraw allowed the Giants to face the Philadelphia Athletics in the 1905 World Series. Hall of Famer Christy Mathewson tossed a 3–0 shutout in the opener, but the Athletics bounced back as "Chief" Bender shutout the Giants 3–0 in Game Two. Those were the last runs that the Athletics would score in the Series. Mathewson threw a 9–0 shutout in Game Three, and Joe McGinnity tossed a 1–0 shutout in Game Four. Mathewson threw his third shutout of the Series in Game Five as the Giants clinched the 1905 World Series Championship.

Every game was a shutout, and the Athletics scored a record low of three runs in the Series. Not only that, the three runs that the Athletics scored in Game Two were all unearned. Thus, the Giants pitching staff recorded an ERA of 0.00 for the Series.

⚾ ⚾ ⚾

Who pitched the most innings in a World Series?

In 1903 Pittsburgh Pirates right-hander Deacon Phillippe out-dueled Boston Pilgrims legend Cy Young in the opener of the inaugural World Series. Pilgrims right-hander Bill Dinneen tossed a shutout in Game Two to even up the Series. An ailing Pirates pitching staff forced Phillippe back into action for Games Three and Four, and he responded with two more complete-game victories. Phillippe became the first and only pitcher to register consecutive complete-game victories in a World Series, but he showed signs of tiring as he surrendered three ninth-inning runs in Game Four.

The heavily favored Pirates had a 3–1 Series lead, but the Pilgrims bounced back, winning Games Five and Six to tie up the Series. In Game Seven, Phillippe pitched his fourth complete game of the Series, but lost to his nemesis Young as the Pilgrims took a one-game lead in the best-of-nine series. Phillippe returned again in Game Eight, but lost the deciding contest, despite having tossed his fifth complete game. Phillippe's record-setting 44 innings in a World Series has lasted more than a century, but it was the Pilgrims who won baseball's first Fall Classic.

⚾ ⚾ ⚾

In how many World Series has the home team won every game?

The Minnesota Twins had the home-field advantage in the 1987 World Series. Games One and Two were played at the Minnesota Metrodome and the Twins won both contests. The Cardinals bounced back, winning games Three, Four, and Five in St. Louis'

Busch Memorial Stadium. The clubs returned to the Metrodome, with its deafening crowd noise, where the Twins won Games Six and Seven, clinching their first World Series Championship. It was the first time in the history of the Fall Classic that the home team won every game in a World Series.

The Twins returned to the World Series in 1991 and faced the Atlanta Braves. The Twins won the first two games at the Metrodome, before dropping Games Three, Four, and Five to the Braves at Atlanta-Fulton County Stadium. History repeated itself when the Twins won Games Six and Seven at the Metrodome. On only two occasions in the history of the Fall Classic has the home team been victorious in every game of a World Series, and the Twins won both of those Series.

$$\oplus \ \oplus \ \oplus$$

Who played in three consecutive World Series for three different teams?

Don Baylor holds the major league career record for being hit by a pitch, but he also set an unusual record in the World Series. In 1986 Baylor was the designated hitter for the Boston Red Sox. The Red Sox won the American League Eastern Division Championship, and faced the California Angels in the ALCS. The Angels had a commanding 3–1 Series lead, and led 5–2 in the top of the ninth inning of Game Five. Baylor hit a clutch ninth-inning homer as the Red Sox rallied to tie the score and win in extra innings. The Red Sox also won Games Six and Seven, clinching the ALCS. Baylor and the Red Sox lost to the Mets in the '86 World Series.

Baylor was traded on September 1, 1987 to the Minnesota Twins, who were on their way to winning the AL Western Division Championship. The Twins defeated the Detroit Tigers in the '87 ALCS and went up against the St. Louis Cardinals. The Cardinals led the Series 3–2, but the Twins returned to the friendly confines of the Metrodome. In Game Six, Baylor hit a clutch home run as the Twins rallied from a 5–2 fifth-inning deficit, and defeated the Cardinals to tie the Series. The Twins prevailed in Game Seven, giving Minnesota its first World Series Championship. Baylor won his first and only World Series ring.

At the end of the season, Baylor signed a one-year contract to play with the Oakland Athletics. The move turned out well for Baylor as the Athletics won their division, and swept the Red Sox in the 1988 ALCS. The American league champions would face the Los Angeles Dodgers in the World Series. Baylor was used sparingly in the '88 Series, and the Athletics fell in five games to the Dodgers. Nonetheless, he played in three consecutive World Series for three different teams.

Is he safe or out? Los Angeles Dodger base runner Bill Sudakis slides into second base as St. Louis Cardinals third baseman Mike Shannon comes from his position to cover the open base. Umpire John Kibler (left) called the runner out while umpire Ed Vargo (right) simultaneously called him safe. Kibler's ruling stood. (Bettmann/Corbis)

Chapter Six

Baseball Puzzlers

When asked if he preferred
Astroturf or grass, Tug McGraw
replied: "I don't know. I never
smoked Astroturf."

Can a dead man strike out?

Baseball is rich with possibilities. Plays that seem impossible can occur at anytime in a game. Fortunately no dead man has struck out, but it could happen. Consider the following: A batter is down two strikes in the count, and his manager decides to bring in a pinch-hitter. The outraged batter goes into the dugout and passes away on the spot. Immediately after this unfortunate turn of events, the pinch-hitter strikes out. The rulebook states: "When the batter leaves the game with two strikes against him, and the substitute batter completes a strikeout, charge the strikeout and the time at-bat to the first batter" (see rule 10.17[b]). The dead player, unbeknownst to him, has struck out.

How can a player score a run without being in the game?

Based on today's rules, if a player leaves the game for any reason, he is prohibited from returning to action. But prior to the 1950 season, teams were allowed a "Courtesy Runner." A courtesy runner was a player permitted to enter the game temporarily as a pinch-runner for an injured teammate. There was no official rule regarding courtesy runners and their entry into the game need not have been noted in the box score. Nonetheless, such runners were allowed whenever the opposing manager gave his permission.

The opposing manager ordinarily chose the courtesy runner and typically would select the slowest player on the opposing team. A courtesy runner would be removed from the game after his injured teammate returned to action. But any courtesy runner, unlike an official pinch-runner, was allowed to return later in the contest. If the courtesy runner stole a base or was caught stealing, then the runner would be credited the steal or charged with the caught stealing. But if the courtesy runner came home, then the original runner was credited with having scored the run.

Consider the following game: On September 23, 1901, Cincinnati Reds outfielder Sam Crawford tripled against right-hander Jim Hughes of the Brooklyn Superbas (who later became the Dodgers). Unfortunately, Crawford was injured as he took third base. The manager of the Superbas allowed Heinie Peitz to enter the game as a courtesy runner. Peitz came in to score but Crawford was credited with having "scored" the run.

$$\oplus \quad \oplus \quad \oplus$$

How can a pitcher give up an earned run without increasing his ERA?

This can happen only if the pitcher has an ERA of "infinity." A hurler can have an ERA of infinity only if he gives up at least one run and never records an out. If a pitcher gives up a home run to the one and only batter he faced in his career, then he will have an ERA of infinity. If he continues to give up more earned runs without registering an out, then his ERA remains at infinity. A few pitchers have ended their career with an ERA of infinity after having faced only one batter, but Cleveland Indians right-hander Elmer "Doc" Hamaan faced the most batters in registering a career ERA of infinity.

On September 21, 1922, the Indians were trailing the Boston Red Sox 9–5 in the ninth inning when Hamaan made his major league debut. The rookie walked the first two batters he faced and hit the following batter with a pitch to load the bases. He walked one more hitter to force in a run. Red Sox outfielder Elmer Miller then drove in three runs with a triple, and that was followed by a single which scored Miller. Another run scored as a result of a wild pitch and a single. Hamaan faced seven batters without registering an out and gave up six earned runs. Finally, manager Tris

Speaker mercifully removed Hamaan from the game. It turned out to be Hamaan's only big league appearance, and he ended his career with an ERA of infinity.

🏐 🏐 🏐

How can a run be both earned and unearned?

An earned run is a run for which a pitcher is held accountable. A pitcher is not charged with an earned run if, for example, a runner who scored reached base as the result of an error (see rule 10.18). In order for a run to be both earned and unearned, a pitching change must occur. Consider the following situation: a starting pitcher gets the first two outs in an inning, but the next batter reaches base as the result of an error. A relief pitcher then enters the game and proceeds to give up a two-run homer. The official scorer must charge one unearned run to the starting pitcher, one earned run to the relief pitcher, and two unearned runs to the team (see rule 10.18 [i]). Thus, the second run is both earned (for the relief pitcher) and unearned (for the team).

🏐 🏐 🏐

How can a batter hit a fair ball over the out-field fence without getting a home run?

Many ballparks had a short right field or left field fence during baseball's formative years. As a result, any batter who hit the ball over the fence wouldn't be credited with a home run unless the fence was a minimum distance from home plate. The following rule was in effect in 1888: "It is a ground-rule double instead of a home run if the ball is batted over the fence in fair territory where the fence is less than 210 feet from home plate" (rule 6.09). In 1892, the rule was amended to 235 feet (rule 6.09). The rule was changed in 1926 to 250 feet (rule 1.04). Minimum distances of at least 250 feet were eventually required of all new ballparks. So it's no longer possible to send a fair ball over the outfield fence without getting credit for a home run.

There is a second answer to this question. In the early part of the 20th century, a game officially ended when the winning run crossed the plate. So if teams were tied entering the bottom of the ninth inning and a player from the home team hit the ball over the fence with a runner on first, then the batter would be credited with a triple. This happened to Babe Ruth on one occasion. On July 18, 1918, the Cleveland Indians visited Fenway Park to play the Boston Red Sox. In the bottom of the ninth of a scoreless tie, Ruth slammed a homer with a runner on first. He was awarded a triple as the Red Sox squeaked out a 1–0 victory.

The Bambino tied for the American League lead in homers that season with 11 round-trippers.

How can a player win the World Series MVP one season and Rookie of The Year the following season?

A player is eligible for World Series play if he's on the team's roster prior to September 1. However, a first-year player officially remains a rookie in his second year of play provided that he had fewer than 130 at-bats in his first season. Consider what happened to Los Angeles Dodgers second basemen Steve Sax. Sax played his first game for the Dodgers on August 18, 1981, and was eligible to play in the post-season. The Dodgers won the National League Championship in the strike-shortened season, and defeated the New York Yankees in the '81 World Series. Sax played sparingly in the Series since he was the backup second baseman for Davey Lopes.

Lopes was traded in the off-season, breaking up baseball's longest running infield, and Sax became the Dodgers' regular second baseman. Sax was classified as a rookie for the 1982 season because he had only 119 at-bats in 1981. The Dodgers second baseman batted .282 in his first full season, and set a Dodgers rookie record with 49 stolen bases. He was named to the National League All-Star team, and was voted NL Rookie of the Year. So, Sax didn't win the World Series MVP one year, and Rookie of the Year the following season, but it was possible.

How can a pitcher throw six consecutive balls to a batter without giving up a base on balls?

A little imagination might help with this question. Let's say a batter comes to the plate with a man on first base and two out. The pitcher starts off with three consecutive balls, but after the third ball is thrown, the runner from first is picked off or caught stealing for the final out of the inning. The batter had a 3-and-0 count but the inning is over. Let's assume that in the next inning, the same pitcher is on the mound and the same batter comes to the plate. If the pitcher throws three more pitches out of the strike zone, then he has thrown six straight balls to the same batter without giving up a walk—provided that the batter does something other than take ball four.

⚾ ⚾ ⚾

How can a pitcher walk a batter without throwing a pitch?

An understanding of baseball's rules is needed to answer this puzzler. Imagine a starting pitcher "brings his pitching hand to his mouth or lips while in the 18-foot circle surrounding the pitching rubber" (rule 8.02 [a] [1]). The rule states that the penalty for this violation is that the umpire shall immediately call a ball. If a stubborn pitcher brings his pitching hand to his mouth or lips once again, then the count will go to 2–0. One unlikely possibility is that the pitcher does the same thing two more times, thereby resulting in a base on balls.

A more likely scenario is that the umpire ejects the pitcher from the game after his second "illegal" pitch. Let's say the count is 2–0, and a reliever throws two additional balls to the batter. Who is charged with the base on balls? The rulebook states that "A relief pitcher shall not be held accountable when the first batter to whom he pitches reaches first base on four called balls if such a batter has a decided advantage in the ball and strike count when pitchers are changed" (see rule 10.18[h]).

Given that the count was either 2–0 or 2–1, the official scorer must charge the original pitcher with a base on balls despite the fact that he never threw a pitch to the batter.

How many hits can a team get in an inning without scoring a run?

It shouldn't be too difficult to figure out how a team can get five hits in an inning without scoring, but the answer is "six." How could it happen? Imagine a leadoff batter gets a base hit and is picked off, caught stealing, or thrown out trying to get an extra base. If the second batter suffers the same fate, we now have the bases empty with two out. Imagine further that the next three batters get singles without a runner scoring. If the following batter gets a hit, then a run should score. Not necessarily. Let's say a batted ball makes contact with one of the base runners. Provided that the runner is not touching one of the bases, the batter is credited with a single, but the runner is ruled out and no runs score. We now have six hits in the inning without a run scoring. It hasn't happened yet.

🔵 🔵 🔵

Can an umpire eject a player from the game and then change his mind?

When an umpire throws a player out of the game, that player is usually gone for good regardless of the merit of his complaint. Nonetheless, umpires have the discretion to change their rulings. Consider the following game: On August 4, 1999, Kansas City Royals visited the Anaheim Angels and umpire Tim Tschida was behind the plate. Angels leadoff batter Orlando Palmeiro struck out in the bottom of the first and subsequently threw his bat to the ground.

Tschida reacted angrily at the apparent disrespect and ejected Palmeiro from the game. Angels manager Terry Collins protested and explained to Tschida that Palmeiro wasn't trying to show him up, but was simply following a recommendation from batting coach Rod Carew. The Angels were in a slump and Carew tried to loosen up the players by having the entire lineup use the same bat throughout the game. That was the reason Palmeiro threw the bat to the ground. Tschida reversed his own ruling and allowed Palmeiro to stay in the game.

The umpiring crew and opposing managers discuss ground rules before a big game. In the early twentieth century, fans were permitted to stand behind ropes on the field of play when stadiums were filled to capacity. As a result, special ground rules had to be put in place. (Bettmann/Corbis)

The Good Old Rules

*"I made a game effort to argue, but
two things were against me: the
umpires and the rules."*
—Leo Durocher

"Runners may be out by 'plugging' them with the
ball, meaning the ball is thrown at the runners to put
them out"("The Rules of the Massachusetts Game
[Town Ball]," Rule 14, May 13, 1858).

In 1870: "The batter is given the privilege of calling
for a low or high pitch" ("The Knickerbocker Rules").

An 1876 rule stated that "If an umpire is unable to
see that a catch is fairly made, he may confer with spec-
tators and players."

In 1878: "There are nine balls in a walk" (see rule 6.08A).

"Any member refusing obedience to his Captain, in the exercise of legal authority, shall pay a fine of 50 cents" ("The Knickerbocker Rules").

In 1879: "There are eight balls in a walk" (see rule 6.08A).

"A spectator who 'hisses or hoots' at or insults the umpire may be ejected from the grounds" (see rule 9.01E).

An 1879 rule stated that "The pitcher is required to face the batter when he pitches" (see rule 8.01).

In 1880: "There are seven balls in a walk" (see rule 6.08).

A 1903 rule stated, "If there is only one umpire in a game, he may stand anywhere on the field he likes" (see rule 9.03[a]).

In 1884: "There are six balls in a walk" (see rule 6.08).

"The bat may have one flattened side" (see rule 1.01).

"In the case of fire, panic, or storm, the umpire does not have to wait until the pitcher has the ball on the mound to call a timeout" (see rule 9.04).

In 1886: "There are five balls in a walk" (see rule 6.08).

A 1920 rule stated that "After he has acquired legal possession of a base, a runner may not run the bases in reverse order for the purpose of confusing the fielders or making a travesty of the game" (see rule 7.08[I]).

In 1889: "There are four balls in a walk" (see rule 6.08A).

Bibliography

Charlton, James, ed. *The Baseball Chronology*. New York, NY: Macmillan Publishing Company, 1991.

Nemec, David, et al., eds. *20th Century Baseball Chronicle*. Lincolnwood, Ill: Publications International Ltd., 1992.

Official Baseball Rules. St. Louis, MO: The Sporting News Publishing Company, 1995.

Pietrusza, David, Matthew Silverman and Michael Gershman, eds. *Baseball: The Biographical Encyclopedia*. Kingston, NY: Total Sports Publishing, 2000.

Shouler, Ken. *Books of Fabulous Facts and Awesome Trivia*. New York, NY: Quill, 2001.

Shouler, Ken. *The Real 100 Best Baseball Players of All Time...And Why*. Lenexa, KA: Addax Publishing, 1998.

Name Index

Books Available
from Santa Monica Press

American Hydrant
by Sean Crane
176 pages $24.95

The Book of Good Habits
Simple and Creative Ways to
Enrich Your Life
by Dirk Mathison
224 pages $9.95

The Butt Hello
and other ways my cats
drive me crazy
by Ted Meyer
96 pages $9.95

Can a Dead Man Strike Out?
Mark S. Halfon
168 pages $11.95

Childish Things
by Davis & Davis
96 pages $19.95

Discovering the History of
Your House
and Your Neighborhood
by Betsy J. Green
288 pages $14.95

The Dog Ate My Resumé
by Zack Arnstein and Larry
Arnstein
192 pages $11.95

Dogme Uncut
Lars von Trier, Thomas Vinterberg and
the Gang That Took on Hollywood
by Jack Stevenson
312 pages $16.95

Exotic Travel Destinations for
Families
by Jennifer M. Nichols
and Bill Nichols
360 pages $16.95

Footsteps in the Fog
Alfred Hitchcock's San Francisco
by Jeff Kraft and
Aaron Leventhal
240 pages $24.95

Free Stuff & Good Deals for
Folks over 50, 2nd Ed.
by Linda Bowman
240 pages $12.95

How to Find Your Family Roots
and Write Your Family History
by William Latham and
Cindy Higgins
288 pages $14.95

How to Speak Shakespeare
by Cal Pritner and
Louis Colaianni
144 pages $16.95

How to Win Lotteries,
Sweepstakes, and Contests in the
21st Century, 2nd Edition
by Steve "America's Sweepstakes
King" Ledoux
224 pages $14.95

Jackson Pollock:
Memories Arrested in Space
by Martin Gray
216 pages $14.95

James Dean Died Here
The Locations of America's Pop Culture
Landmarks
by Chris Epting
312 pages $16.95

The Keystone Kid
Tales of Early Hollywood
by Coy Watson, Jr.
312 pages $24.95

The Largest U.S. Cities Named
after a Food
by Brandt Maxwell
360 pages $16.95

Letter Writing Made Easy!
Featuring Sample Letters for Hundreds
of Common Occasions
by Margaret McCarthy
224 pages $12.95

Letter Writing Made Easy!
Volume 2
Featuring More Sample Letters for
Hundreds of Common Occasions
by Margaret McCarthy
224 pages $12.95

Life is Short. Eat Biscuits!
by Amy Jordan Smith
96 pages $9.95

Loving Through Bars
Children with Parents in Prison
by Cynthia Martone
208 pages $21.95

Marilyn Monroe Dyed Here
More Locations of America's
Pop Culture Landmarks
by Chris Epting
312 pages $16.95

Movie Star Homes
by Judy Artunian and
Mike Oldham
312 pages $16.95

Offbeat Museums
The Collections and Curators of
America's Most Unusual Museums
by Saul Rubin
240 pages $19.95

A Prayer for Burma
by Kenneth Wong
216 pages $14.95

Quack!
Tales of Medical Fraud from the
Museum of Questionable Medical
Devices
by Bob McCoy
240 pages $19.95

Redneck Haiku
by Mary K. Witte
112 pages $9.95

School Sense: How to Help
Your Child Succeed in
Elementary School
by Tiffani Chin, Ph.D.
408 pages $16.95

Silent Echoes
Discovering Early Hollywood Through
the Films of Buster Keaton
by John Bengtson
240 pages $24.95

Tiki Road Trip
A Guide to Tiki Culture in
North America
by James Teitelbaum
288 pages $16.95

Order Form 1-800-784-9553

	Quantity	Amount
American Hydrant ($24.95)	_____	_____
The Book of Good Habits ($9.95)	_____	_____
The Butt Hello . . . and Other Ways My Cats Drive Me Crazy ($9.95)	_____	_____
Can a Dead Man Strike Out? ($11.95)	_____	_____
Childish Things ($19.95)	_____	_____
Discovering the History of Your House. . . ($14.95)	_____	_____
The Dog Ate My Resumé ($11.95)	_____	_____
Dogme Uncut ($16.95)	_____	_____
Exotic Travel Destinations for Families ($16.95)	_____	_____
Footsteps in the Fog: Alfred Hitchcock's San Francisco ($24.95)	_____	_____
Free Stuff & Good Deals for Folks over 50, 2nd Ed. ($12.95)	_____	_____
How to Find Your Family Roots . . . ($14.95)	_____	_____
How to Speak Shakespeare ($16.95)	_____	_____
How to Win Lotteries, Sweepstakes, and Contests . . . ($14.95)	_____	_____
Jackson Pollock: Memories Arrested in Space ($14.95)	_____	_____
James Dean Died Here: America's Pop Culture Landmarks ($16.95)	_____	_____
The Keystone Kid: Tales of Early Hollywood ($24.95)	_____	_____
The Largest U.S. Cities Named after a Food ($16.95)	_____	_____
Letter Writing Made Easy! ($12.95)	_____	_____
Letter Writing Made Easy! Volume 2 ($12.95)	_____	_____
Life is Short. Eat Biscuits! ($9.95)	_____	_____
Loving Through Bars ($21.95)	_____	_____
Marilyn Monroe Dyed Here ($16.95)	_____	_____
Movie Star Homes ($16.95)	_____	_____
Offbeat Museums ($19.95)	_____	_____
A Prayer for Burma ($14.95)	_____	_____
Quack! Tales of Medical Fraud ($19.95)	_____	_____
Redneck Haiku ($9.95)	_____	_____
School Sense ($16.95)	_____	_____
Silent Echoes: Early Hollywood Through Buster Keaton ($24.95)	_____	_____
Tiki Road Trip ($16.95)	_____	_____

		Subtotal	_____
Shipping & Handling:		CA residents add 8.25% sales tax	_____
1 book	$3.00	Shipping and Handling (see left)	_____
Each additional book is	$ .50	**TOTAL**	_____

Name _____

Address _____

City _____ State _____ Zip _____

☐ Visa ☐ MasterCard Card No.: _____

Exp. Date _____ Signature _____

☐ Enclosed is my check or money order payable to:

Santa Monica Press LLC
P.O. Box 1076
Santa Monica, CA 90406
www.santamonicapress.com 1-800-784-9553